I AND THOU

I AND THOU

Martin Buber

A NEW TRANSLATION
WITH A PROLOGUE "I AND YOU"
AND NOTES

BY

WALTER KAUFMANN

CHARLES SCRIBNER'S SONS

NEW YORK

CONTENTS

ACKNOWLEDGMENTS

THE PRESENT VOLUME owes its existence to Rafael Buber. In June 1969 he phoned me from Boston, explained that he was Martin Buber's son, and asked whether he could come to see me in Princeton. We had never met, and he offered no explanation; but when he came a few days later, there was an instant rapport, coupled with an intriguing lack of directness. He told me of his desire for a new English translation of *Ich und Du* and asked my counsel. I recalled how his father had told me that he considered Ronald Gregor Smith, who had done *I and Thou*, by far his best translator. Rafael insisted that those whose advice he valued were agreed that the old version had to be replaced. I myself had attacked the use of "thou" instead of "you" in print, but at this point did not let on that I did not like the old translation. Instead I pointed out how nearly untranslatable the book was. Rafael did not protest, but his mind was made up, and he wanted my help. I mentioned names. They would not do: the new version had to be done by someone who had been close to his father; and he had come a long way and did not want to return home to Israel without having accomplished this mission. Now I insisted that the book really was untranslatable, and that all one could do was to add notes, explaining plays on words—and I gave an example. Instant agreement: that was fine—a translation with notes. He wanted me to do it, however I chose to do it, and it was clear that I would have his full cooperation.

This I got. That unforgettable day in my study, and later on in the garden, was the fourth anniversary of Martin Buber's death. I hesitated for a few days, but the challenge proved irresistible. Thus I was led back into another dialogue with Martin Buber, well over thirty years after I had first seen and heard him in Lehnitz (between Berlin and Oranienburg) where he had come with Ernst Simon at his side to teach young people *Bibel lesen*—to read the Bible.

In the summer of 1969 I visited the Buber Archive in Jerusalem and had a look at the handwritten manuscript of *Ich und Du* and at Buber's correspondence with Ronald Gregor Smith. I asked for copies of the complete manuscript and of all pages on which Buber had commented on points of translation. The material was promptly sent to me and turned out to be of considerable interest. (See the Key, below.) Having noticed some discrepancies between the first edition of the book and the later editions, I asked Rafael Buber whether he had a record of the variants. He did not, but made a list himself, by hand, for my use.

Both from him and from Mrs. Margot Cohn, who for decades was Buber's secretary and who now works full-time in the Archive, I have encountered not only kindness and cooperation at every point but the spirit of friendship.

I have been equally fortunate with my undergraduate research assistant at Princeton, Richard L. Smith '70. He had read the original translation of *I and Thou* three times before he began to assist me, and he loved the book. There is no accounting for how many times he has read it now, comparing the new version with the old one, raising questions, compiling the glossary, and reading proofs. Working with him has been a delight.

Siegwart Lindenberg, assisting me in two courses in 1969-70, very kindly went over the new translation during the semester break and compared it with the German text. His queries and suggestions have been immensely helpful, and it was wonderful to be able to discuss some of the most difficult passages with a friend.

KEY

IN THE NOTES there are numerous references to "Buber, March 1937," followed by hitherto unpublished information. This material comes from Buber's letters to Ronald Gregor Smith, who made the first translation of *Ich und Du.*

After reading the page proofs of that version, Buber requested well over two hundred corrections. Many involved serious misunderstandings. As soon as I had completed my version, I checked Buber's criticisms to make sure that mistakes pointed out in March 1937 had not been reintroduced unwittingly. It was a strange experience to find my readings of many difficult passages confirmed by Buber, years after his death.

Occasionally he offered glosses that went beyond the German text and explained more fully what had been in his mind. These self-interpretations, not previously available in any language, are included in the notes and identified: "Buber, March 1937."

"Before 1957" identifies variants between the first and second editions. Many of these changes are too slight to affect the translation or to be worth recording here. Thus *Wörterpaars* became *Wortpaars; Eines* was changed to *eines;* and *um dich herum, um dich her.* All the more substantial revisions are indicated in the notes.

I AND YOU

A PROLOGUE

by

Walter Kaufmann

I

Man's world is manifold, and his attitudes are manifold. What is manifold is often frightening because it is not neat and simple. Men prefer to forget how many possibilities are open to them.

They like to be told that there are two worlds and two ways. This is comforting because it is so tidy. Almost always one way turns out to be common and the other one is celebrated as superior.

Those who tell of two ways and praise one are recognized as prophets or great teachers. They save men from confusion and hard choices. They offer a single choice that is easy to make because those who do not take the path that is commended to them live a wretched life.

To walk far on this path may be difficult, but the choice is easy, and to hear the celebration of this path is pleasant. Wisdom offers simple schemes, but truth is not so simple.

Not all simplicity is wise. But a wealth of possibilities breeds dread. Hence those who speak of many possibilities speak to the few and are of help to even fewer. The wise offer only two ways, of which one is good, and thus help many.

*

Mundus vult decipi: the world wants to be deceived. The truth is too complex and frightening; the taste for the truth is an acquired taste that few acquire.

Not all deceptions are palatable. Untruths are too easy to come by, too quickly exploded, too cheap and ephemeral to give lasting comfort. *Mundus vult decipi;* but there is a hierarchy of deceptions.

Near the bottom of the ladder is journalism: a steady

stream of irresponsible distortions that most people find refreshing although on the morning after, or at least within a week, it will be stale and flat.

On a higher level we find fictions that men eagerly believe, regardless of the evidence, because they gratify some wish.

Near the top of the ladder we encounter curious mixtures of untruth and truth that exert a lasting fascination on the intellectual community.

What cannot, on the face of it, be wholly true, although it is plain that there is some truth in it, evokes more discussion and dispute, divergent exegeses and attempts at emendations than what has been stated very carefully, without exaggeration or onesidedness. The Book of Proverbs is boring compared to the Sermon on the Mount.

*

The good way must be clearly good but not wholly clear. If it is quite clear, it is too easy to reject.

What is wanted is an oversimplification, a reduction of a multitude of possibilities to only two. But if the recommended path were utterly devoid of mystery, it would cease to fascinate men. Since it clearly should be chosen, nothing would remain but to proceed on it. There would be nothing left to discuss and interpret, to lecture and write about, to admire and merely think about.

The world exacts a price for calling teachers wise: it keeps discussing the paths they recommend, but few men follow them. The wise give men endless opportunities to discuss what is good.

*

Men's attitudes are manifold. Some live in a strange world bounded by a path from which countless ways lead inside. If there were road signs, all of them might bear the same inscription: I-I.

Those who dwell inside have no consuming interest. They are not devoted to possessions, even if they prize some; not to people, even if they like some; not to any project, even if they have some.

Things are something that they speak of; persons have the great advantage that one cannot only talk *of* them but also *to*, or rather *at* them; but the lord of every sentence is no man but I. Projects can be entertained without complete devotion, spoken of, and put on like a suit or dress before a mirror. When you speak to men of this type, they quite often do not hear you, and they never hear you as another I.

You are not an object for men like this, not a thing to be used or experienced, nor an object of interest or fascination. The point is not at all that you are found interesting or fascinating instead of being seen as a fellow I. The shock is rather that you are not found interesting or fascinating at all: you are not recognized as an object any more than as a subject. You are accepted, if at all, as one to be spoken at and spoken of; but when you are spoken of, the lord of every story will be I.

*

Men's attitudes are manifold. Some men take a keen interest in certain objects and in other men and actually think more about them than they think of themselves. They do not so much say I or think I as they do I.

They "take" an interest, they do not give of themselves.

They may manipulate or merely study, and unlike men of the I–I type they may be good scholars; but they lack devotion.

This I-It tendency is so familiar that little need be said about it, except that it is a tendency that rarely consumes a man's whole life. Those who see a large part of humanity —their enemies, of course—as men of this type, have succumbed to demonology.

This is merely one of the varieties of man's experience and much more widespread in all ages as a tendency and much rarer as a pure type in our own time than the Manichaeans fancy.

*

There are men who hardly have an I at all. Nor are all of them of one kind.

Some inhabit worlds in which objects loom large. They are not merely interested in some thing or subject, but the object of their interest dominates their lives. They are apt to be great scholars of extraordinary erudition, with no time for themselves, with no time to have a self.

They study without experiencing: they have no time for experience, which would smack of subjectivity if not frivolity. They are objective and immensely serious. They have no time for humor.

They study without any thought of use. What they study is an end in itself for them. They are devoted to their subject, and the notion of using it is a blasphemy and sacrilege that is not likely to occur to them.

For all that, their "subject" is no subject in its own right, like a person. It has no subjectivity. It does not speak to them. It is a subject one has chosen to study—one of the subjects that one may legitimately choose, and there may be others working on the same subject, possibly on a slightly different aspect of it, and one respects them insofar as they, too, have no selves and are objective.

Here we have a community of solid scholars—so solid that there is no room at the center for any core. Theirs is the world of It-It.

*

There are other ways of having no I. There are men who never speak a sentence of which I is lord, but nobody could call them objective. At the center of their world is We.

The contents of this We can vary greatly. But this is an orientation in which I does not exist, and You and It and He and She are only shadows.

One type of this sort could be called We-We. Theirs is a sheltered, childish world in which no individuality has yet emerged.

*

Another perennial attitude is summed up in the words Us-Them. Here the world is divided in two: the children of light and the children of darkness, the sheep and the goats, the elect and the damned.

Every social problem can be analyzed without much study: all one has to look for are the sheep and goats.

There is room for anger and contempt and boundless hope; for the sheep are bound to triumph.

Should a goat have the presumption to address a sheep, the sheep often do not hear it, and they never hear it as another I. For the goat is one of Them, not one of Us.

Righteousness, intelligence, integrity, humanity, and victory are the prerogatives of Us, while wickedness, stupidity, hypocrisy, brutality, and ultimate defeat belong to Them.

Those who have managed to cut through the terrible complexities of life and offer such a scheme as this have been hailed as prophets in all ages.

*

In these five attitudes there is no You: I-I, I-It, It-It, We-We, and Us-Them. There are many ways of living in a world without You.

There are also many worlds with the two poles I-You.

*

I-You sounds unfamiliar. What we are accustomed to is I-Thou. But man's attitudes are manifold, and Thou and You are not the same. Nor is Thou very similar to the German *Du*.

German lovers say *Du* to one another, and so do friends. *Du* is spontaneous and unpretentious, remote from formality, pomp, and dignity.

What lovers or friends say Thou to one another? Thou is scarcely ever said spontaneously.

Thou immediately brings to mind God; *Du* does not. And the God of whom it makes us think is not the God to whom one might cry out in gratitude, despair, or agony, not the God to whom one complains or prays spontaneously: it is the God of the pulpits, the God of the holy tone.

When men pray spontaneously or speak directly to God, without any mediator, without any intervention of formulas, when they speak as their heart tells them to speak instead of repeating what is printed, do they say Thou? How many know the verb forms Thou commands?

The world of Thou has many mansions. Thou is a preachers' word but also dear to anticlerical romantic poets. Thou is found in Shakespeare and at home in the English Bible, although recent versions of the Scriptures have tended to dispense with it. Thou can mean many things, but it has no place whatever in the language of direct, nonliterary, spontaneous human relationships.

If one could liberate I-Thou from affectation, the price for that would still involve reducing it to a mere formula, to jargon. But suppose a man wrote a book about direct relationships and tried to get away from the formulas of theologians and philosophers: a theologian would translate it and turn *Ich und Du* into *I and Thou*.

II

Men love jargon. It is so palpable, tangible, visible, audible; it makes so obvious what one has learned; it satisfies the craving for results. It is impressive for the uninitiated. It makes one feel that one belongs. Jargon divides men into Us and Them.

Two books appeared during the same year. One was called *Ich und Du*, the other *Das Ich und das Es*. Rarely have two books of such importance had such simple names.

Both books proposed three central concepts: the former also *Es*, the latter also *Über-ich*. But neither book was trinitarian in any profound sense. Both were dualistic. The wise emphasize two principles.

Freud's *Ich* was the conscious part of the soul, his *Es* the unconscious part, and his *Über-ich* a third part which he also called the *Ich-Ideal* or the conscience. But it was part of his central concern at that time to go "Beyond the Pleasure Principle" and introduce a second basic drive.

Buber could also have called his book *Das Ich und das Es.*
He could also have spoken of an *Über-ich*, or perhaps an
Über-du. But he was not speaking of parts of the soul. He
singled out two relationships: that in which I recognize It
as an object, especially of experience and use, and that in
which I respond with my whole being to You. And the last
part of his book dealt with the divine You.

Men love jargon. In English one book became *I and
Thou* and the other *The Ego and the Id.* Thus even people
who had not read these books could speak of ego, id, and
superego, of the I-Thou and the I-It.

Actually, Freud had written his most epoch-making
books before *Das Ich und das Es,* without using these terms,
and his system did not depend on these words. That never
deterred those who loved to speak and write about the ego
and the id.

Buber wrote many later works in which he did not harp
on *Ich* and *Du.* He was not a man of formulas but one who
tried to meet each person, each situation, and each subject
in its own way. That never deterred those who loved to
speak and write about "the I-It" and "the I-Thou."

*

There are many modes of I-You.

Kant told men always to treat humanity, in our person
as well as that of others, as an end also and never only as
a means. This is one way of setting off I-You from I-It. And
when he is correctly quoted and the "also" and the "only"
are not omitted, as they all too often are, one may well
marvel at his moral wisdom.

Innumerable are the ways in which I treat You as a
means. I ask your help, I ask for information, I may buy

from you or buy what you have made, and you sometimes dispel my loneliness.

Nor do I count the ways in which You treat me as a means. You ask my help, you ask me questions, you may buy what I have written, and at times I ease your loneliness.

Even when you treat me *only* as a means I do not always mind. A genuine encounter can be quite exhausting, even when it is exhilarating, and I do not always want to give myself.

Even when you treat me *only* as a means because you want some information, I may feel delighted that I have the answer and can help.

But man's attitudes are manifold, and there are many ways of treating others as ends *also*. There are many modes of I-You.

You may be polite when asking; you may show respect, affection, admiration, or one of the countless attitudes that men call love.

Or you may not ask but seek without the benefit of words. Or you may speak but not ask, possibly responding to my wordless question. We may do something together. You may write to me. You may think of writing to me. And there are other ways. There are many modes of I-You.

The total encounter in which You is spoken with one's whole being is but one mode of I-You. And it is misleading if we assimilate all the other modes of I-You to I-It.

*

Philosophers tend to reduce the manifold to the twofold. Some of the greatest taught that there were two worlds. Why has hardly anyone proclaimed many worlds?

We have heard of the two ways of opinion and knowledge, the two realms of appearance and reality, this world and the other, matter and mind, phenomena and noumena, representation and will, nature and spirit, means and end, It and You.

Side by side with technical philosophy similar games are played. Naïve and sentimental poets have been contrasted in a lengthy and immensely influential essay that has left its mark on subsequent discussions of the classical and the romantic. Later on the Apollinian and the Dionysian emerged as a variant. And the It and You.

The straight philosophers tend to celebrate one of the two worlds and depreciate the other. The literary tradition is less Manichaean. Friedrich Schiller tried to comprehend both kinds of poetry without disparaging either naïve or sentimental tendencies, and Nietzsche followed his example in his early contrast of the two Greek gods.

Ich und Du stands somewhere between the literary and philosophical traditions. Buber's "It" owes much to matter and appearance, to phenomena and representation, nature and means. Buber's "You" is the heir of mind, reality, spirit, and will, and his I-You sometimes has an air of Dionysian ecstasy. Even if I-It is not disparaged, noboby can fail to notice that I-You is celebrated.

*

The year before *Ich und Du* appeared, Leo Baeck published a major essay on *Romantische Religion* that was meant to be the first part of a larger work on "Classical and Romantic Religion." Eventually, it became the capstone of his *Judaism and Christianity.*

The theme: "We encounter two forms above all, classical and romantic religiousness, classical and romantic religion . . . Judaism and Christianity."

Baeck's apologetics is inspiring, his polemic is inspired.

But after a hundred pages one is bound to ask oneself if his procedure is not unsound.

Even where the two notions played off against each other in endless variations are not black and white, one is led to wonder eventually if the play impulse has not got out of hand, if repetition has not replaced argument, and virtuosity demonstration.

Certainly, Buber's delight in language gets between him and his readers. There might as well be a screen between them on which one watches the antics of his words instead of listening to him. The words do tricks, the performance is brilliant, but much of it is very difficult to follow.

Obscurity is fascinating. One tries to puzzle out details, is stumped, and becomes increasingly concerned with meaning—unless one feels put off and gives up altogether.

Those who persevere and take the author seriously are led to ask about what he could possibly have meant, but rarely seem to wonder or discuss whether what he says is true.

Instead of asking how things are in fact, and how one could possibly find out, one wonders mostly whether one has got the author's point; and if one thinks one has, one may even feel superior to those who have not.

Speaking in Kierkegaard's terms, one might say that Buber makes it all too easy for his readers to avoid his ethical challenge by adopting an aesthetic orientation. Precisely the same might be said of Kierkegaard himself.

III

Success is no proof of virtue. In the case of a book, quick acclaim is presumptive evidence of a lack of substance and originality.

Most books are stillborn. As the birthrate rises steeply,

infant mortality soars. Most books die unnoticed; fewer live for a year or two.

Those that make much noise when they see the light of day generally die in childhood. Few books live as long as fifty years. For those that do, the prognosis is good: they are likely to live much longer than their authors.

In the case of a book, longevity is presumptive evidence of virtue, although survival usually also owes a good deal to a book's vices. A lack of clarity is almost indispensable.

*

Books that survive their authors do not weather time like rocks. They are reborn without having quite died and have several overlapping lives. Some fall asleep in one country, come to life in another, and then wake up again.

Ich und Du was fourteen years old when it began a new life in the English-speaking world as *I and Thou*, in 1937. The next year the author left Germany for Jerusalem, and the German book seemed to be headed for death at fifteen.

In his new home Buber did not meet with the acclaim that he had won from German Jewry in the years of persecution. No longer could he write in German. He had to try his hand at Hebrew. And people joked that he did not yet know Hebrew well enough to write as obscurely as he had written in German.

*

I and Thou survived, mainly among Protestant theologians. That a book by a man who felt so strongly about being a Jew should have been acclaimed primarily by Protestants has struck many people as ironical. What is much more remarkable is that a sharp attack on all talk about God and all pretensions to knowledge about God—a sustained attempt to rescue the religious dimension of life from the theologians—should have been received so well by theologians. They generously acclaimed Buber as a Jewish theologian, and went right on doing what they had done. Only now their discourse was enriched with frequent references to the I-Thou and the I-It.

After World War II the book gained a far wider hearing, especially in Germany, where it was rediscovered, and in the United States. After the holocaust a widespread need was felt to love and admire a representative Jew. The competition was not keen. There was no dearth of great writers and scientists who were Jews, but what was wanted was a representative and teacher of the Jewish tradition—a contemporary heir, if that were possible, of the Hebrew prophets.

In the twentieth century neither Eastern European Jewry nor American Jewry had produced such figures, while the German Jews, whom both of these far larger communities tended to regard with some resentment, could point to several. Franz Rosenzweig, with whom Buber had undertaken a new German translation of the Hebrew Bible, had died in 1929. But even after World War II there were still Baeck and Buber.

Baeck, too, gained another hearing now. But when the war ended he was in his seventies and, having spent the last part of the war in Theresienstadt, somewhat frail. Moreover, his manner had always been exceedingly refined, and he was a rabbi. He was an immensely impressive person, and the rabbinical students who sat at his feet at Hebrew Union College where he came to teach one semester a year will never forget him any more than those who heard him lecture in Frankfurt a few months before his death— tall, stooped, and undaunted; over eighty; speaking without notes, as brilliantly as in his prime. Here was greatness, but it belonged to a past period of history, almost to a vanished civilization. He spoke of rebirth on that occasion and, back from Theresienstadt, youthful in old age, symbolized it. But those who learned from him did not feel that he was one of them.

Martin Buber's personal appearances in Germany and the United States were different. He was very small, not at all likely to be noticed from far away; and his bearing did not create a sense of distance. Nor was he a brilliant lecturer—at least not in this last phase. Unlike Baeck, whose eyesight was so poor that he had trained himself to get along without notes, Buber often read long papers that most of the audience could not follow. But as soon as the lecture was over and the questions started, he stood revealed as the exceptional man he was. If there was any ostentation now, it was in his insistence on establishing genuine dialogue. What was unforgettable was the attempt to triumph over distance; to bridge differences in age, cultural background, and language; to listen and communicate. And those who knew him tried to keep him from lecturing in the first place and have discussion from the start. But these discussions were not ordinary. On such occasions *I and You* became incarnate.

*

Never was the popularity of Buber's little masterpiece as great as it became after his death. This posthumous triumph probably owed little to his personality. It was part of a larger wave.

It took Kant and Hegel a few decades to arrive in the United States. It took the German 1920's forty years.

Kafka arrived sooner. But he was almost unknown in

Germany when he died in 1924; he did not belong to the German twenties as much as did Hesse and Buber, Heidegger and Brecht.

Buber's immense posthumous popularity is not confined to him. Those who read *I and Thou* also read Hesse's *Steppenwolf* and talk of Heidegger, usually without having read him, just as students did in Germany in the twenties. This goes with a sexual revolution and an interest in drugs, a vast enthusiasm for Dostoevsky, Indian philosophy, and Buddhism. The whole syndrome has come to life again along with interest in Bertolt Brecht whose antisentimental and antiromantic protests have to be seen against the background of a time that acclaimed Hesse and Buber. His toughness has some of the swagger of adolescent rebellion. But their neo-romanticism also had, and still has, a particular appeal for adolescents. A book's survival usually owes not a little to its vices.

*

Our first loves leave their mark upon us. In the crucial years of adolescence I loved Hesse's novels and experienced Buddhism and Indian wisdom as a great temptation to detachment. Buber taught me that mysticism need not lead outside the world. Or if mysticism does, by definition, so much the worse for it.

It was from Buber's other writings that I learned what could also be found in *I and Thou:* the central commandment to make the secular sacred.

Ich und Du I did not read in my teens, and later the style of this little book put me off as much as its dualism. Even more than Nietzsche's *Zarathustra,* it is overwritten. We are far from the clear, crisp air of a sunny autumn morning in the mountains and the bracing wit of Nietzsche's later prose. We seem even further from the simplicity of Kafka's style, schooled on the Book of Genesis.

Yet few books of our century equal the economy of Buber's *Tales of the Hasidim*. There he reached perfection. Among his own writings, *The Way of Man According to the Teachings of Hasidism* is a work of comparable beauty that distils Buber's own teaching in less than twenty pages.* It is also Buber's best translated work, but he neither recalled nor was able to find out who had translated it.

The style of *Ich und Du* is anything but sparse and unpretentious, lean or economical. It represents a late flowering of romanticism and tends to blur all contours in the twilight of suggestive but extremely unclear language. Most of Buber's German readers would be quite incapable of saying what any number of passages probably mean.

The obscurity of the book does not seem objectionable to them: it seems palpable proof of profundity. Sloth meets with awe in the refusal to unravel mysteries.

And the Hasidic tradition meets with the conventions of German philosophy in endowing teachers with an aura of authority. In this ambience it is not for the student to challenge or to examine critically. One tries to absorb what one can and hopes to understand more in the future.

This world may be gone, but modern art and poetry, plays and films have predisposed Buber's readers once again not to ask what every detail means. One has come to suspect reasons and analysis and feels ready for Zen, for Indian wisdom, and for Buber's book.

It is not even impossible that in places Buber himself was not sure of the exact meaning of his text. One of the last things he wrote was a long reply to twenty-nine mostly friendly critics who had collaborated on a volume on his work that appeared first in German (*Martin Buber*, 1963)

*It is reprinted, uncut, in my *Religion from Tolstoy to Camus*.

and then also in English (*The Philosophy of Martin Buber*, 1967). His response, printed at the end of the volume, also contains some discussion of *Ich und Du;* and here Buber says: "At that time I wrote what I wrote under the spell of an irresistible enthusiasm. And the inspirations of such enthusiasm one may not change any more, not even for the sake of exactness. For one can only estimate what one would gain, but not what would be lost."

Thus Buber endowed his own text with authority and implied that he himself could not tell its full meaning. Any attempt to clarify dark passages might eliminate pertinent associations. It should be clear where that leaves the translator!

IV

It may be doubted whether the style of the book really communicates the force of inspiration. In places the aesthetic surface of the book looks like mere *Schöngeisterei;* the style seems mannered, the plays on words at best clever, and those who hate affectation may even wonder whether this virtuosity hides a lack of content. In fact, it hides a profoundly antiromantic message.

The content may *appear* to be as romantic as the form. Of the many possible relationships in which I encounter You as another I, Buber singles out a state that is almost ecstatic. As long as we focus on this choice, we are almost bound to see him as a romantic and to miss his import.

Buber's most significant ideas are not tied to his extraordinary language. Nor do they depend on any jargon. On the contrary, they cry out to be liberated from all jargon.

The sacred is here and now. The only God worth keeping is a God that cannot be kept. The only God worth

talking about is a God that cannot be talked about. God is
no object of discourse, knowledge, or even experience. He
cannot be spoken of, but he can be spoken to; he cannot
be seen, but he can be listened to. The only possible relationship with God is to address him and to be addressed
by him, here and now—or, as Buber puts it, in the present.
For him the Hebrew name of God, the tetragrammaton
(YHVH), means HE IS PRESENT. *Er ist da* might be translated:
He is there; but in this context it would be more nearly
right to say: He is here.

Where? After Auschwitz and Nagasaki, where? We look
around and do not see him. But he is not to be seen. Never.
Those who have claimed to see him did not see him.

Does he really address us? Even if we wanted to, desper-
ately, could we listen to him? Does he speak to us?

On the first page of the original edition of the book one
was confronted by only two lines:

> *So hab ich endlich von dir erharrt:*
> *In allen Elementen Gottes Gegenwart.*

"Thus I have finally obtained from you by waiting / God's
presence in all elements." No source was indicated, but
this epigraph came from Goethe's *West-östlicher Divan*. It
brings to mind Goethe's contemporary, William Blake:

> To see a World in a Grain of Sand
> And a Heaven in a Wild Flower
> Hold Infinity in the palm of your hand
> And Eternity in an Hour.

But in Buber's book the emphasis actually does not fall on
all elements; and that is surely one reason why he omitted
the epigraph in 1957. Asked why he had deleted it, he said:
Because it could be misunderstood. And in the later editions of some early works he also changed some phrases

that had a pantheistic ring. But in 1923, when *Ich und Du* appeared with the epigraph from Goethe, Buber also published a collected edition of some earlier "Lectures on Judaism" (*Reden über das Judentum*), adding a Foreword that makes clear his desire even at that time to distinguish his own position from any pantheism.

We must ask to whom the "you" (*dir*) in the epigraph had been meant to refer. In Goethe's *Divan* the lines occur in the short dialogue that concludes "The Innkeeper's Book" (*Das Schenkenbuch*), and the innkeeper is addressing the poet. This dialogue, incidentally, was added only after the original edition. But of whom could Buber have been thinking? *Ich und Du* bore no dedication; but the sequel, *Zwiesprache* (1932: Dialogue) was dedicated to Buber's wife, Paula, with a four-line verse:

> *An P.*
> *Der Abgrund und das Weltenlicht,*
> *Zeitnot und Ewigkeitsbegier,*
> *Vision, Ereignis und Gedicht:*
> *Zwiesprache wars und ists mit dir.*

"For P. The abyss and the light of the world, / Time's need and the craving for eternity, / Vision, event, and poetry: / Was and is dialogue with you."

Thus the epigraph in *Ich und Du* may be understood as a "concealed dedication" to Paula Buber, who in 1921 had published a book in which the elements, which had been pagan in her previous work, were full of God.* The motto

---

*I owe the phrase in quotes, this interpretation, and most of the information about the epigraph to Grete Schaeder, who will argue her case in her introduction to the first volume of Buber's correspondence. I don't know whether she has noticed that the two lines in the *Divan* that follow upon Buber's epigraph support her reading: *Wie du mir das so lieblich gibst! / Am lieblichsten aber dass du liebst:* "How you give this to me in such a lovely way! But what is loveliest is that you love."

could scarcely be understood as it was meant. But rightly understood, it serves notice that the book was grounded in an actual relationship between a human I and a human You.

The centrality of human relationships in this book is so plain that critics have actually noted with surprise and protested with complete incomprehension that there should be any mention at all of a tree and of a cat. The central stress falls on You—not Thou. God is present when I confront You. But if I look away from You, I ignore him. As long as I merely experience or use you, I deny God. But when I encounter You I encounter him.

*

For those who no longer have any use for the word "God" this may be too much; and for those who do, too little. But is it too little?

> When you come to appear before me,
>   who requires of you
>   this trampling of my courts?
> Bring no more vain offerings;
>   incense is an abomination to me.
> New moon and sabbath and the calling of assemblies—
>   I cannot endure iniquity and solemn assembly.
> Your new moon and your appointed feasts
>   my soul hates;
> they have become a burden to me,
>   I am weary of bearing them.
> When you spread forth your hands,
>   I hide my eyes from you;
> even though you make many prayers,
>   I no longer listen;
>   your hands are full of blood.

Wash yourselves; make yourselves clean;
    remove the evil of your doings
    from before my eyes;
cease to do evil,
    learn to do good;
seek justice,
    correct oppression;
defend the fatherless,
    plead for the widow.

Is that too little?

*

Nor is it too much. In places it seems a bit much. Buber seems so dramatic, so insistent on what seems obvious. But there are self-refuting prophecies, and Hebrew prophecy was not meant to come true.

The Hebrew prophets foretold disasters that would come to pass unless those who heard them returned from their evil ways. Jeremiah did not gloat when Jerusalem was destroyed; he was grieved by his failure.

Jonah, of course, felt aggrieved when his prophecy forestalled its own fulfillment; but this only provides the occasion for the moral of the story. He is told, and we are told, that this sort of failure is a triumph.

If Buber places so much stress on what seems obvious to me, one has to ask in fairness whether it would seem so obvious if he had not been so insistent on it.

When a religion professor makes a great point of treating students as persons, that seems almost comical. How else? But when every student who comes to my office to speak to me, and everyone who asks a question of me during or after a lecture comes to life for me as an I addressing me and I try to speak not *about him* but *to You*

—would it be that way but for the influence of Martin Buber?

I am not sure and I will never know. The loves of childhood and of adolescence cannot be subtracted from us; they have become part of us. Not a discrete part that could be severed. It is as if they had entered our blood stream.

*

Nevertheless, if one has no use for the word "God" it may seem merely obscurantist to make this point in this fashion. Why not say instead that we ought to be mindful that the human beings we confront are persons?

It still seems hard not to reply: what else could they be? isn't this obvious? In any case, Buber says more than this, without saying too much.

He finds in my encounter with You what Blake finds in a grain of sand and in a wild flower: infinity and eternity —here and now.

Far better than John Dewey who tried something similar in *A Common Faith*, Buber succeeds in endowing the social sphere with a religious dimension. Where other critics of religion tend to take away the sabbath and leave us with a life of weekdays, Buber attacks the dichotomy that condemns men to lives that are at least six-sevenths drab.

While man cannot live in a continual sabbath, he should not resign himself to a flat two-dimensional life from which he escapes on rare occasions. The place of the sacred is not a house of God, no church, synagogue, or seminary, nor one day in seven, and the span of the sacred is much shorter than twenty-four hours. The sabbath is every day, several times a day.

*

Still why use religious terms? Indeed, it might be better not to use them because they are always misunderstood. But what other terms are there?

We need a new language, and new poets to create it, and new ears to listen to it.

Meanwhile, if we shut our ears to the old prophets who still speak more or less in the old tongues, using ancient words, occasionally in new ways, we shall have very little music.

We are not so rich that we can do without tradition. Let him that has new ears listen to it in a new way.

*

In Buber's little book God actually does not appear much before the Third Part. But a heretic need not consider that last part embarrassing or *de trop.* On the contrary.

Those without ties to organized religion who feel that, although much of institutional religion is repulsive, not all scriptures are bare nonsense, have to ask themselves: what about God?

Those who prefer the God of Abraham, Jacob, and Job to the God of the philosophers and theologians have to ask: what about God?

Those who read the Bible and the Sacred Books of the East not merely as so much literature but as a record of experiences that are relevant to their own lives must ask: what about God?

They do not ask: what is he really like? what are his attributes? is he omniscient? can he do this or that? Nor: can his existence be proved? They do not assume that they

know him and only need one additional piece of information. They do not even believe in him. What they ask about
is not some supernatural He. And the theologians are of
little help, if any.

If only one knew the meaning of one's own question! If
only one could ask it properly or formulate it more precisely! Is it really a question? Or is it a deep concern that
finds no words that do it justice?

This book responds to this concern. God as the eternal
You whom men address and by whom they in turn feel—
Buber would say, *are*—addressed makes sense of much
literature and life. The book does not save, or seek to prop
up, a tradition. Even less does it aim to save any institution.
It speaks to those who no longer believe but who wonder
whether life without religion is bound to lack some dimension.

V

The book is steeped in Judaism. This is often overlooked
and perhaps as often denied explicitly. Jesus is mentioned,
as is the Gospel according to John; but so are the Buddha
and the Upanishads. The author is widely read, conversant
with many traditions—a modern intellectual with deep
roots in the German language. The volume abounds in
coinages, but it is difficult to be quite sure in any case
whether a particular word is really a coinage: so thorough
was Buber's knowledge of German literature, all the way
back to Luther and even Eckhart and beyond. He was far
from any orthodoxy, far even from being conservative in
almost any sense of that word. Of labels of that sort, even
radical would fit him better.

He was possessed by the desire to get back to the roots.

His handling of the language makes that plain at every turn. And when he resolved to translate the Hebrew Bible with Franz Rosenzweig, he found a fertile field for this great passion. For in Hebrew it could be argued that one did not really understand a word until one had grasped its root and considered its relations to other words with the same root.

The whole endeavor of translating the Hebrew Bible represented an attempt to get back to the roots of Judaism —back beyond the roots of Christianity. Buber sought a way back beyond the Shtetl and the Shulhan Arukh, back beyond the Talmud and the Mishnah, even beyond Ezra and Nehemiah. He went to the roots in the prophets and in Moses, and in some ways his own Judaism was pre-Mosaic.

The Greeks were an eminently visual people. They gloried in the visual arts; Homer's epics abound in visual detail; and they created tragedy and comedy, adding new dimensions to visual art.

The Hebrews were not so visual and actually entertained a prohibition against the visual arts. Neither did they have tragedies or comedies. The one book of the Bible that has sometimes been called a tragedy, Job, was clearly not intended for, and actually precluded, any visual representation.

The Greeks visualized their gods and represented them in marble and in beautiful vase paintings. They also brought them on the stage.

The Hebrews did not visualize their God and expressly forbade attempts to make of him an object—a visual object, a concrete object, any object. Their God was not to be seen. He was to be heard and listened to. He was not an It but an I—or a You.

•

Modern Christian attempts to get back to a pre-Hellenistic primal Christianity are legion. They are also doomed.

There never was any pre-Hellenistic Christianity. The soil on which Christianity was born had soaked up Hellenism for more than three centuries. Paul wrote his epistles in Greek, and he was a Hellenistic Jew—a Jew, to be sure, and deeply beholden to Judaism, but a Hellenistic Jew and not by any stretch of the imagination a pre-Hellenistic Jew. And the four Gospels were written in Greek somewhat later than were Paul's epistles.

Christianity was born of the denial that God could not possibly be seen. Not all who considered Jesus a great teacher became Christians. Christians were those for whom he was the Lord. Christians were those who believed that God could become visible, an object of sight and experience, of knowledge and belief.

Of course, Christianity did not deny its roots in Judaism. Jesus as the Son of God who had ascended to the heavens to dwell there with God, as God, did not simply become another Heracles, the son of Zeus who had ascended to the heavens to dwell there with the gods, as a god. He did not simply become another of the legion of Greek gods and demigods and sons of Zeus. He had preached and was to be heard and listened to. His moral teachings were recorded lovingly for the instruction of the faithful.

But were they really to be listened to? Or did they, too, become objects—of admiration and perhaps discussion? Was the individual to feel addressed by them, commanded by them—was he to relate his life to them?

The new dispensation was hardly that. The New Testament keeps saying, nowhere more emphatically than in the Gospel according to John, that those who only live by

Jesus' moral teaching shall not enter the kingdom of heaven; only those can be saved who are baptized, who believe, and who take the sacraments—eating, as that Gospel puts it, "of this bread."

Of course, Christian belief is not totally unlike Jewish belief. It is not devoid of trust and confidence, and in Paul's and Luther's experience of faith these Jewish elements were especially prominent. Rarely have they been wholly lacking in Christianity. Still, this Jewish faith was never considered sufficient. Christian faith was always centered in articles of faith that had to be believed, and disputes abounded about what precisely had to be believed by those who wanted to be saved.

When the Reformation did away with visual images, it was only to insist more firmly on the purity of doctrines that must be believed. And for Luther the bread and wine were no mere symbols of Christ's flesh and blood—otherwise he might have made common cause with Ulrich Zwingli and prevented the splintering of Protestantism—but the flesh and blood itself: God as an object.

Buber does not say these things, and I have no wish to saddle him with my ideas. His views are developed in his *Two Types of Faith*, mine in my *Critique of Religion and Philosophy* and *The Faith of a Heretic*. Why introduce these problems here? Because the notion of so many Christians and some Jews that Buber was really closer to Christianity than he was to Judaism should not go unchallenged. In fact, *Ich und Du* is one of the great documents of Jewish faith.

*

One of the central concepts of the book is that of *Umkehr*. This is Buber's German rendering of the Hebrew

t'shuvah and means return. The noun is found in the Bible,
but not in the distinctive sense which is common in Jewish
literature and liturgy. The verb is frequently used in the
Bible with the connotations that are relevant here:
Deuteronomy 4:30 and 30:2, Isaiah 10:21 and 19:22, and
Jeremiah 4:1 are among the many examples. What is
meant is the return to God.

The modern reader is apt to feel that this is a churchly
notion, presumably dear to preachers but without significance for those who do not greatly care for organized
religion. In fact, the idea is quite unecclesiastical and it
constitutes a threat to organized religion. Christianity in
particular is founded on its implicit denial.

The Jewish doctrine holds that a man can at any time
return and be accepted by God. That is all. The simplicity
of this idea is deceptive. Let us translate it into a language
closer to Christianity, while noting that Buber refrains
from doing this: God can at any time forgive those who
repent.

What the Hebrew tradition stresses is not the mere state
of mind, the repentance, but the act of return. And on
Yom Kippur, the Day of Atonement, the Book of Jonah is
read in synagogues the world over. When Jonah had cried
out, "Yet forty days, and Nineveh shall be overthrown,"
the king called on his people "to return, every man, from
his evil way and from the violence on his hands. Who
knows, God may return . . ." Nineveh was the capital of
the Assyrians who had conquered the kingdom of Israel,
laid waste Samaria, and led the ten tribes away into de-
struction. Could God possibly forgive them without at
least demanding their conversion and some ritual observ-
ances? "When God saw what they did, how they returned
from their evil way, God repented of the evil that he had
said he would do to them and did it not."

This conception of return has been and is at the very heart of Judaism, and it is for the sake of this idea that Jonah is always read on the highest holiday of the year. But the theology of Paul in the New Testament is founded on the implicit denial of this doctrine, and so are the Roman Catholic and the Greek Orthodox churches, Lutheranism and Calvinism. Paul's elaborate argument concerning the impossibility of salvation under the Torah ("the Law") and for the necessity of Christ's redemptive death presuppose that God cannot simply forgive anyone who returns.

If the doctrine of the return is true, Paul's theology collapses and "Christ died in vain." Nor does any need remain for baptism and the sacrament of confession, or for the bread and the wine. Man stands in a direct relationship to God and requires no mediator.

Buber's whole book deals with such immediate relationships, and in this as well as in his central emphasis on return he speaks out of the Jewish religious tradition.

It was both a symptom and then also a cause of profound incomprehension that in the first English translation *Umkehr* became reversal. Twenty years later, in the second edition, this was changed to "turning." Meanwhile the choice of "Thou" did its share to make God remote and to lessen, if not destroy, the sense of intimacy that pervades Buber's book.

*

Buber's lifelong Zionism was prompted in large measure by his concern for the creation of a new way of life and a new type of community. His Zionism has been called cultural rather than political, but it was not altogether unfitting that when he finally went to Jerusalem in 1938 it was to accept an appointment to a new chair in Social

Philosophy in the Hebrew University's Department of Sociology. (He was first offered the chair of Pedagogy and declined it.)

The recurrent "Thou" in the first translation mesmerized people to the point where it was widely assumed that Buber was a theologian. In fact, the book deals centrally with man's relationships to other men, and the theme of alienation (*Verfremdung*) is prominent in the Second Part.

The aim of the book is not to disseminate knowledge about God but, at least in large measure, to diagnose certain tendencies in modern society—Buber speaks of "sick ages" more than forty years before it became fashionable in the West to refer to our "sick" society—and to indicate how the quality of life might be changed radically by the development of a new sense of community.

The book will survive the death of theology, for it appeals to that religiousness which finds no home in organized religion, and it speaks to those whose primary concern is not at all with religion but rather with social change.

But there is much more to the book than this.

*

Among the most important things that one can learn from Buber is how to read. Was it from him that I learned it? I am not sure, and I will never know. Does it matter? *You* could learn it from this book.

Modern man is a voracious reader who has never learned to read well. Part of the trouble is that he is taught to read drivel that is hardly worth reading well. (There was a time when Jewish children learned to read by reading the Bible.)

One ends up by reading mainly newspapers and magazines—ephemeral, anonymous trash that one scans on its way to the garbage can. One has no wish to remember it for any length of time; it is written as if to make sure that one won't; and one reads it in a manner that makes doubly sure. There is no person behind what one reads; not even a committee. Somebody wrote it in the first place—if one can call that writing—and then various other people took turns changing it. For the final result no one is responsible; and it rarely merits a serious response. It cries out to be forgotten soon, like the books on which one learned to read, in school. They were usually anonymous, too; or they should have been.

In adolescence students are suddenly turned loose on books worth reading, but generally don't know how to read them. And if, untaught, some instinct prompts them to read well, chances are that they are asked completely tone-deaf questions as soon as they have finished their assignment—either making them feel that they read badly after all or spoiling something worthwhile for the rest of their lives.

We must learn to feel addressed by a book, by the human being behind it, as if a person spoke directly to us. A good book or essay or poem is not primarily an object to be put to use, or an object of experience: it is the voice of You speaking to me, requiring a response.

How many people read Buber or Kierkegaard that way? Nietzsche or Hegel? Tolstoy or Euripides? Or the Bible? Rather, how few do? But Buber himself wants to be read that way.

VI

One can also learn from Buber how to translate. Nowhere is his teaching more radical. Nowhere is he more deeply at odds with the common sense of the English-speaking world.

Nor did anything he ever published seem as absurd to his readers in Germany as did his translation of the Bible. What was familiar seemed to have become incomprehensible.

In the beginning all this was due at least as much to Rosenzweig's uncompromising nature as to Buber, but Buber persisted even after Rosenzweig's death, and neither ridicule nor criticism ever moved him to relent. When he left Germany in 1938, the vast undertaking that had required so much effort looked like an almost total loss.

After the war, Buber was delighted when two German publishers asked him to resume his enterprise. He did, and brought it to completion shortly before his death. Gershom Scholem, a great scholar whose view of Hasidism differs from Buber's, toasted the accomplishment, adding: But who will read it?

What had seemed outrageous in the twenties and thirties was merely ahead of its time. A new generation that no longer expects all prose and poetry to be so easily accessible finds no extraordinary difficulty with the Buber Bible. It is widely read in Germany.

What can be learned from Buber as a translator before one explores devices and techniques is the basic commitment to the writer one translates. As a translator I have no right to use the text confronting me as an object with which I may take liberties. It is not there for me to play with or manipulate. I am not to use it as a point of departure, or as anything else. It is the voice of a person that needs me. I am there to help him speak.

If I would rather speak in my own voice, I am free to do that—on other occasions. To foist my thoughts, my images, my style on those whom I profess to translate is dishonest.

Mundus vult decipi. The world winks at dishonesty. The world does not call it dishonesty.

In the case of poetry it says: what is most important is that the translator should write a poem that is good in its own right. The acceptance of this absurdity by so many intellectuals helps us to understand the acceptance of so many absurd religious and political beliefs by intellectuals in other times and climes. Once a few respected men have fortified a brazen claim with their prestige, it becomes a cliché that gets repeated endlessly as if it were self-evident. Any protest is regarded as a heresy that shows how those who utter it do not belong: arguments are not met on their merits; instead one rehearses a few illustrious names and possibly deigns to contrast them with some horrible examples.

Anyone able to write a poem that is good in its own right should clearly do so, but he should not pass it off as a translation of another man's poem if the meaning or the tone of his poem are in fact quite different. Least of all should he claim that the tone or meaning is the same when it is not.

Tone is crucial and often colors meaning. If we don't know what is said seriously and what in jest, we do not know the meaning. We have to know what is said lightly and what solemnly, where a remark is prompted by a play on words, if something is ironical or a quotation, an allusion, a pastiche, a parody, a diatribe, a daring coinage, a cliché, an epigram, or possibly ambiguous.

A German translator who rendered William Faulkner into the equivalent of the King's English would serve his public ill. But if he tried hard to be faithful to his author, then his publisher might say to him—if things were as they are in the United States: "My dear fellow, that simply isn't German"; and an editor, utterly unable to write a single publishable page over his—or more often her—own name, would be asked to rewrite the translation to make it "idiomatic."

Ah, we are told, every generation needs its own translation because a book has to be done into the idiom of the day. If it is poetry, it had better sound like Eliot. Alas, no more; we need a new translation. But why should Goethe, Hölderlin, or Rilke sound like Eliot in the first place? Should Eliot, conversely, have been made to sound like Rilke—and then perhaps like Brecht—and now like someone whom a publisher or critic fancies as a modern voice?

The point of reading a poet is surely in large measure to hear *his* voice—his own, distinctive, novel voice. Poetry read in the original stands a better chance of being read well than prose. But when we deal with translations, the roles are reversed.

Again I do not want to saddle Buber with my own views. What he translated was Scripture. Perhaps I am *extending* the lessons one could learn from him—and from Rosenzweig, who also translated ninety-two hymns and poems by Yehuda Halevi, with a brilliant postscript, and dedicated the book to Martin Buber. The point is not to invoke Buber as an authority but rather to spell out some of the implications of this book.

*

Buber ought to be translated as he translated. The voice should be his, the thoughts and images and tone his. And if the reader should cry out, exasperated, "But that simply isn't English," one has to reply: "True, but the original text simply isn't German." It abounds in solecisms, coinages, and other oddities; and Buber was a legend in his lifetime for the way he wrote.

He makes very difficult reading. He evidently did not wish to be read quickly, once only, for information. He tried to slow the reader down, to force him to read many sentences and paragraphs again, even to read the whole book more than once.

The style is not the best part of this book, but it is a part and even an important part of it. Nobody has to chew passage upon passage more slowly than a translator who takes his work seriously and keeps revising his draft. Nobody has occasion to ask himself more often whether a play on words really adds something worthwhile. But once he starts making an effort to improve upon his text, keeping only the most brilliant plays on words while leaving out and not calling attention to inferior ones, possibly substituting his own most felicitous plays for the ones he could not capture, where is he to stop on the road to falsehood?

When adjectives are piled up in profusion and some strike him as decidedly unnecessary, should he substitute a single forceful word for a two-line enumeration? Make long and obscure sentences short and clear? Resolve all ambiguities in favor of the meaning he likes best? Gloss over or leave out what seem weaknesses to him? Perhaps insert a few good images that the author might have liked if only he had thought of them, and that perhaps would have occurred to him if he had written his book in English, and if he had shared more of the translator's background —and sensibility? Perhaps add a thought or two as well?

The book has many faults. Let him that can write a better one do so with all haste. But to meddle with a text one translates and to father one's inventions on another man is a sin against the spirit.

*

What one should try to do is clear. What can be done is something else again. This book is untranslatable.

It abounds in plays on words—don't call them plays if that should strike you as irreverent—that simply cannot be done into English. How can one translate the untranslatable?

By adding notes. By occasionally supplying the German words. By offering explanations.

But now the text seems much less smooth. One is stopped in one's tracks to read a note. One is led to go back to reread a paragraph. And having read the book with so many interruptions, one really has to read it a second time without interruptions.

To quote Rilke's "Song of the Idiot": How good!

*

Some of the key terms in this book are hard to render. Examples abound in the notes. Here it must suffice to comment on a few points.

Buber loves the prefix *Ur*, which has no exact English equivalent. An *Urgrossvater* is a great-grandfather; an *Ururgrossvater*, a great-great-grandfather. *Urwald* is forest primeval; *Ursprung*, origin. These are common words, but the prefix opens up endless possibilities for coinages. In the following pages it has been rendered by "primal."

Buber also loves the suffix *haft* (for adjectives)—and *haftigkeit* (for nouns). This can have two altogether different connotations. It can mean "having": thus *lebhaft* means vivacious (literally: having life); *launenhaft*, moody (having moods); and *tugendhaft*, virtuous (having virtue). But it can also mean "somewhat like": *märchenhaft* means fabulous (somewhat like a fairytale). This suffix opens up endless possibilities for coinages, and occasionally it is not altogether clear which of the two meanings is intended. Usually, Buber definitely intends the second: he adds the suffix to introduce a lack of precision or, to put the matter more kindly, to stress the inadequacy of language.

One of his favorite words is *Gegenwart*, which can mean either the present, as opposed to the past and the future, or presence, as it does when he speaks of God's presence in the epigraph to the first edition. The German language does not distinguish between these two senses of the word; nor does Buber. To add to this difficulty, "present" is ambiguous in English: it can also mean "gift." In the following pages "present" is never used in that sense. Like "presence" it is used exclusively to render *Gegenwart*.

Gegen means against but also figures as a prefix in a great many words; and Buber uses a number of these. *Gegenstand* is the ordinary German word for object (literally that which stands against). *Gegenüber* means vis-à-vis (literally that which is over against), and this in turn can become a prefix and figures in many different constructions. In this book "confront" has been used in all such cases. *Begegnung* (noun) and *begegnen* (verb) have been translated consistently as encounter. The list could be continued, but there is no need here to anticipate the notes.

Buber's persistent association of *Wirklichkeit* with *wirken* can be carried over into English to some extent by using "actuality" for the former (saving "reality" for the rare instances when he uses *Realität*) and "act," in a variety of ways, for the verb. And when he says that in prayer we can, incredible as it may seem, *wirken* on God, although of course we cannot *erwirken* anything from him, the translator can say that we can act on God but not exact anything from him.

*

One of Buber's most central terms is *Wesen.*

The word is not uncommon, and those who know a little about German philosophic terms know that it means essence. They also know that Buber has sometimes been called an existentialist, and that some other philosophers have been called, more rarely, essentialists. But in this book *Wesen* recurs constantly. Sometimes "essence" is clearly what is meant; sometimes "nature" would be slightly more idiomatic; but quite often neither of these terms makes any sense at all.

Wesen can also mean "a being" or, when the context indicates that it is used in the plural, "beings." To complicate matters further, we sometimes encounter *Wesenheiten,* a much more unusual word that it would be easy to do without; but Buber shows a preference for rare words and coinages.

Any contrast of essence and existence is out of the picture. Deliberately so. Every being I encounter is seen to be essential. Nothing is essential but a being. Doing something with my whole being or my whole essence is the same.

The realm of essences and what is essential is not outside this world in some beyond. Essential is whatever is—here and now.

*

If romanticism is flight from the present, yearning for deliverance from the cross of the here and now, an escape into the past, preferably medieval, or the future, into drugs or other worlds, either night or twilight—if romanticism can face anything except the facts—then nothing could be less romantic than the central appeal of this book.

Hic Rhodos, hic salta!

"Here is Rhodes; jump here!" That is what Aesop's braggart was told when he boasted of his great jump in Rhodes.

Hegel cited this epigram in the preface to his *Philosophy of Right* by way of contrasting his approach and Plato's. He was not trying to instruct the state how it ought to be: "To comprehend *what is*, is the task of philosophy, for *what is* is reason. . . . Slightly changed, the epigram would read [seeing that *rhodon* is the Greek word for rose]:

Here is the rose, dance *here*. . . .

To recognize reason as the rose in the cross of the present and thus to delight in the present—this rational insight brings us that *reconciliation* with actuality which philosophy grants those who have once been confronted by the inner demand to *comprehend . . .* "

To link Buber with Hegel may seem strange. But in 1920 Franz Rosenzweig had published a major work, in two volumes, on "Hegel and the State," dealing at length with this preface. The differences between Buber and Hegel far outnumber their similarities. But they are at one in their opposition to any otherworldliness, in their insistence on finding in the present whatever beauty and redemption there may be, and in their refusal to pin their hopes on any beyond.

Ich und Du speaks to men and women who have become
wary of promises and hopes: it takes its stand resolutely in
the here and now. It is a sermon on the words of Hillel:

> "If I am only for myself, what am I?
> And if not now, when?"

A PLAN MARTIN BUBER ABANDONED

IN AN ESSAY "On the History of the Dialogical Principle" Buber relates that "the first, still awkward draft of *Ich und Du* dates from the fall of 1919. Originally it was meant to be the first part of a five-volume work, whose contents I had outlined briefly in 1916; but its systematical character estranged me from it before long."*

In the final manuscript of the book, in the Buber Archive in Jerusalem, I found an outline apparently written in 1922, just after the book was finished.** It is reproduced here in translation and in facsimile, with the permission of Ernst Simon and the Archive. Although the rest of the plan was abandoned, it is noteworthy that the three subheadings of "I and You" fit the three parts of our book. I take it that "Word" refers to the two basic words. And in place of "History" the second part could also be entitled "Alienation."

*"Zur Geschichte des dialogischen Prinzips" (1954), in *Werke*, vol. I (1962), p. 298. The whole essay is only thirteen pages long.
**The date was established by Rivka Horwitz in *Buber's Way to I and Thou*, Heidelberg, Lambert Schneider, 1978, pp. 156 and 209.

The significance of the fact that Buber was unable to complete the work is discussed in Walter Kaufmann, *Discovering the Mind*, Volume II: *Nietzsche, Heidegger, and Buber*, New York, McGraw-Hill, 1980, section 46ff.

I AND THOU

I. I and You
1. Word. 2. History. 3. God.

II. Primal Forms of Religious Life
1. Magic. 2. Sacrifice. 3. Mystery. 4. Prayer.

III. Knowledge of God and Law of God
1. Myth. 2. Dogma. 3. Law. 4. Teaching.

IV. Person and Community
1. The Founder. 2. The Priest. 3. The Prophet.
4. The Reformer. 5. The Solitary.

V. The Power and the Kingdom

I. Ich und Du
1. Wort. 2. Geschichte. 3. Gott.

II. Urformen des religiösen Lebens
1. Magie. 2. Das Opfer. 3. Das Mysterium. 4. Das Gebet

III. Gotteskunde und Gottesgesetz
1. Mythus. 2. Dogma 3. Gesetz. 4. Lehre.

IV. Die Person und die Gemeinde
1. Der Stifter. 2. Der Priester. 3. Der Prophet.
4. Der Reformator. 5. Der Einsame

V. Die Kraft und das Reich

Martin Buber's

I AND THOU

First Part

THE WORLD IS TWOFOLD for man in accordance with his twofold attitude.

The attitude of man is twofold in accordance with the two basic words he can speak.

The basic words are not single words but word pairs.

One basic word is the word pair I-You.

The other basic word is the word pair I-It; but this basic word is not changed when He or She takes the place of It.

Thus the I of man is also twofold.

For the I of the basic word I-You is different from that in the basic word I-It.[1]

*

Basic words do not state something that might exist outside them; by being spoken they establish a mode of existence.[2]

[1] In the first edition the next section began: "Basic words do not signify things but relations." This sentence was omitted by Buber in 1957 and in all subsequent editions.

[2] *stiften sie einen Bestand.* The locution is most unusual, and *Bestand* in any applicable sense is very rare. Buber intends a contrast with "that might exist" (*was . . . bestünde*).

Basic words are spoken with one's being.[3]

When one says You, the I of the word pair I-You is said, too.

When one says It, the I of the word pair I-It is said, too.

The basic word I-You can only be spoken with one's whole being.

The basic word I-It can never be spoken with one's whole being.

*

There is no I as such but only the I of the basic word I-You and the I of the basic word I-It.

When a man says I, he means one or the other. The I he means is present when he says I. And when he says You or It, the I of one or the other basic word is also present.

Being I and saying I are the same. Saying I and saying one of the two basic words are the same.

Whoever speaks one of the basic words enters into the word and stands in it.

*

The life of a human being does not exist merely in the sphere of goal-directed verbs. It does not consist merely of activities that have something for their object.

I perceive something. I feel something. I imagine something. I want something. I sense something. I think something. The life of a human being does not consist merely of all this and its like.

All this and its like is the basis of the realm of It.

But the realm of You has another basis.

[3] *Wesen:* see page 46.

*

Whoever says You does not have something for his object. For wherever there is something there is also another something; every It borders on other Its; It is only by virtue of bordering on others. But where You is, said there is no something. You has no borders.

Whoever says You does not have something; he has nothing. But he stands in relation.

*

We are told that man experiences his world. What does this mean?

Man goes over the surfaces of things and experiences them.[4] He brings back from them some knowledge of their condition—an experience. He experiences what there is to things.

But it is not experiences alone that bring the world to man.

For what they bring to him is only a world that consists of It and It and It, of He and He and She and She and It.

I experience something.

[4] *Der Mensch befährt die Fläche der Dinge und erfährt sie.* Both *erfährt* in this sentence and *erfahre* in the preceding paragraph are forms of *erfahren*, the ordinary German equivalent of the verb, to experience. The noun is *Erfahrung.* These words are so common that it has hardly ever occurred to anyone that they are closely related to *fahren*, an equally familiar word that means to drive or go. *Befahren* means to drive over the surface of something. The effect of the German sentence is to make the reader suddenly aware of the possibility that *erfahren* might literally mean finding out by going or driving, or possibly by traveling. But by further linking *erfahren* with *befahren* Buber manages to suggest that experience stays on the surface.

In the original manuscript this point was elaborated further in the sentence immediately following upon this paragraph; but Buber struck it out: "Thus the fisherman gets his catch. But the find is for the diver."

All this is not changed by adding "inner" experiences
to the "external" ones, in line with the non-eternal distinction that is born of mankind's craving to take the edge off
the mystery of death. Inner things like external things,
things among things!

I experience something.

And all this is not changed by adding "mysterious"
experiences to "manifest" ones, self-confident in the wisdom that recognizes a secret compartment in things, re-
served for the initiated, and holds the key. O mysteriousness without mystery, O piling up of information! It,
it, it!

*

Those who experience do not participate in the world.
For the experience is "in them" and not between them and
the world.

The world does not participate in experience. It allows
itself to be experienced, but it is not concerned, for it
contributes nothing, and nothing happens to it.

*

The world as experience belongs to the basic word I-It.
The basic word I-You establishes the world of relation.

*

Three are the spheres[5] in which the world of relation
arises.

The first: life with nature. Here the relation vibrates in

[5]This locution echoes the Passover Haggadah which contains a famous
song in which each stanza begins: One is . . . , Two are . . . , Three are
. . . , etc.

the dark and remains below language. The creatures stir across from us, but they are unable to come to us, and the You we say to them sticks to the threshold of language.

The second: life with men. Here the relation is manifest and enters language. We can give and receive the You.

The third: life with spiritual beings. Here the relation is wrapped in a cloud but reveals itself,[6] it lacks but creates language. We hear no You and yet feel addressed; we answer—creating, thinking, acting: with our being we speak the basic word, unable to say You with our mouth.

But how can we incorporate into the world of the basic word what lies outside language?

In every sphere, through everything that becomes present to us, we gaze toward the train[7] of the eternal You; in each we perceive a breath of it;[8] in every You we address the eternal You, in every sphere according to its manner.

*

I contemplate a tree.

I can accept it as a picture: a rigid pillar in a flood of light, or splashes of green[9] traversed by the gentleness of the blue silver ground.

I can feel it as movement: the flowing veins around the sturdy, striving core, the sucking of the roots, the breathing of the leaves, the infinite commerce with earth and air —and the growing itself in its darkness.

I can assign it to a species and observe it as an instance, with an eye to its construction and its way of life.

I can overcome its uniqueness and form so rigorously

[6] *sich offenbarend.* A few lines earlier, *offenbar* was translated as manifest. The adjective, unlike the verb, generally has no religious overtones.
[7] *Saum* means hem or edge, but this is surely an allusion to Isaiah 6:1.
[8] *Weben:* literally, blowing (of a breeze or wind), wafting.
[9] *das spritzende Gegrün:* the noun is a coinage.

that I recognize it only as an expression of the law—those laws according to which a constant opposition of forces is continually adjusted, or those laws according to which the elements mix and separate.

I can dissolve it into a number, into a pure relation between numbers, and eternalize it.

Throughout all of this the tree remains my object and has its place and its time span, its kind and condition.

But it can also happen, if will and grace are joined, that as I contemplate the tree I am drawn into a relation, and the tree ceases to be an It. The power of exclusiveness has seized me.

This does not require me to forego any of the modes of contemplation. There is nothing that I must not see in order to see, and there is no knowledge that I must forget. Rather is everything, picture and movement, species and instance, law and number included and inseparably fused.

Whatever belongs to the tree is included: its form and its mechanics, its colors and its chemistry, its conversation with the elements and its conversation with the stars—all this in its entirety.

The tree is no impression, no play of my imagination, no aspect of a mood; it confronts me bodily[1] and has to deal with me as I must deal with it—only differently.

One should not try to dilute the meaning of the relation: relation is reciprocity.

Does the tree then have consciousness, similar to our own? I have no experience of that. But thinking that you have brought this off in your own case, must you again

[1] *Er leibt mir gegenüber . . . Leib* means body; *leibt* is most unusual and means literally: it bodies—across from me or vis-à-vis me. Locutions that involve *gegenüber* abound in this book. A few lines below, in the first sentence of the next section, we find *Stehe ich . . . gegenüber;* in the following section, *gegenübertritt* and *des Gegenüber* and—a variant—*entgegentritt.* Cf. p. 45.

divide the indivisible? What I encounter is neither the soul
of a tree nor a dryad, but the tree itself.

*

When I confront a human being as my You and speak
the basic word I-You to him, then he is no thing among
things nor does he consist of things.

He is no longer He or She, limited by other Hes and
Shes, a dot in the world grid of space and time, nor a
condition that can be experienced and described, a loose
bundle of named qualities. Neighborless and seamless, he
is You and fills the firmament. Not as if there were nothing
but he; but everything else lives in *his* light.

Even as a melody is not composed of tones, nor a verse
of words, nor a statue of lines—one must pull and tear to
turn a unity into a multiplicity—so it is with the human
being to whom I say You. I can abstract from him the color
of his hair or the color of his speech or the color of his
graciousness; I have to do this again and again; but immediately he is no longer You.

And even as prayer is not in time but time in prayer, the
sacrifice not in space but space in the sacrifice—and whoever reverses the relation annuls the reality—I do not find
the human being to whom I say You in any Sometime and
Somewhere. I can place him there and have to do this
again and again, but immediately he becomes a He or a
She, an It, and no longer remains my You.

As long as the firmament of the You is spread over me,
the tempests of causality cower at my heels, and the whirl
of doom[2] congeals.

The human being to whom I say You I do not experi-

[2] *Verhängnis* means, and has been consistently translated as, doom;
Schicksal, as fate.

ence. But I stand in relation to him, in the sacred basic
word. Only when I step out of this do I experience him
again. Experience is remoteness from You.

The relation can obtain even if the human being to
whom I say You does not hear it in his experience. For You
is more than It knows. You does more, and more happens
to it, than It knows. No deception reaches this far: here is
the cradle of actual life.

*

This is the eternal origin of art that a human being
confronts a form that wants to become a work through
him. Not a figment of his soul but something that appears
to the soul and demands the soul's creative power. What
is required is a deed that a man does with his whole being:
if he commits it and speaks with his being the basic word[3]
to the form that appears, then the creative power is
released and the work comes into being.

The deed involves a sacrifice and a risk. The sacrifice:
infinite possibility is surrendered on the altar of the form;
all that but a moment ago floated playfully through one's
perspective has to be exterminated; none of it may penetrate into the work; the exclusiveness of such a confrontation demands this. The risk: the basic word can only be
spoken with one's whole being; whoever commits himself
may not hold back part of himself; and the work does not
permit me, as a tree or man might, to seek relaxation in the

---

[3] *Es kommt auf eine Wesenstat des Menschen an: vollzieht er sie, spricht er
mit seinem Wesen das Grundwort* . . . Henceforth, *Wesenstat* and *Wesens-
akt* are translated "essential deed" and "essential act"; but the meaning
that is intended is spelled out here.
"Form": *Gestalt.* One might consider leaving this word untranslated
because *Gestalt* has become familiar in English; but the associations of
Gestalt psychology might be more distracting than helpful, and *Gestal-
tung* (below: "forming") needs to be translated in any case.

It-world; it is imperious: if I do not serve it properly, it breaks, or it breaks me.

The form that confronts me I cannot experience nor describe; I can only actualize it. And yet I see it, radiant in the splendor of the confrontation, far more clearly than all clarity of the experienced world. Not as a thing among the "internal" things, not as a figment of the "imagination," but as what is present. Tested for its objectivity, the form is not "there" at all; but what can equal its presence? And it is an actual relation: it acts on me as I act on it.[4]

Such work is creation, inventing is finding.[5] Forming is discovery. As I actualize, I uncover. I lead the form across —into the world of It. The created work is a thing among things and can be experienced and described as an aggregate of qualities. But the receptive beholder[6] may be bodily confronted now and again.

*

—What, then, does one experience of the You?
—Nothing at all. For one does not experience it.
—What, then, does one know of the You?
—Only everything. For one no longer knows particulars.

---

[4] actual: *wirklich;* acts: *wirkt;* act: *wirke.* Earlier in the same paragraph, actualize: *verwirklichen.* In English "real" and "realize" would sometimes be smoother than "actual" and "actualize"; but it is noteworthy that the German word *wirklich* is so closely associated, not only by Buber but also by Nietzsche and Goethe before him, with *wirken, Werk* (work), *Wirkung* (effect), and *wirksam* (effective). Cf. p. 45f.

[5] *Schaffen ist Schöpfen, Erfinden ist Finden. Schaffen* can mean to work or to create; *schöpfen* means to create. *Erfinden* is the ordinary German word for invent, and *finden* means to find.

[6] *dem . . . Schauenden. Schauen* is a way of looking that in this book is not associated with experiencing, with objects, with It. It has generally been translated "behold."

*

The You encounters me by grace—it cannot be found by seeking. But that I speak the basic word to it is a deed of my whole being, is my essential deed.

The You encounters me. But I enter into a direct relationship to it. Thus the relationship is election and electing, passive and active at once: An action of the whole being must approach passivity, for it does away with all partial actions and thus with any sense of action, which always depends on limited exertions.

The basic word I-You can be spoken only with one's whole being. The concentration and fusion into a whole being can never be accomplished by me, can never be accomplished without me. I require a You to become; becoming I, I say You.

All actual life is encounter.

*

The relation to the You is unmediated.[7] Nothing conceptual intervenes between I and You, no prior knowledge and no imagination; and memory itself is changed as it plunges from particularity into wholeness. No purpose

---

[7] *unmittelbar* is the ordinary German word for immediate. *Mittel* is the ordinary word for means (the noun, both in the contrast of means and ends and also in the sense of being without means). This noun is encountered in the last two sentences of this paragraph. In the first sentence of the following paragraph Buber contrasts *Unmittelbarkeit* and *alles Mittelbare.* In the present context it seemed feasible and important to reproduce this counterpoint of concepts in English, but elsewhere *unmittelbar* has often been translated as direct. While this word is positive and *unmittelbar* is negative, "direct" suggests more forcibly the absence of any intermediary than does "immediate" with its primarily temporal connotations.

intervenes between I and You, no greed and no anticipation; and longing itself is changed as it plunges from the dream into appearance. Every means is an obstacle. Only where all means have disintegrated encounters occur.

*

Before the immediacy of the relationship everything mediate becomes negligible. It is also trifling whether my You is the It of other I's ("object of general experience") or can only become that as a result of my essential deed. For the real boundary, albeit one that floats and fluctuates, runs not between experience and non-experience, nor between the given and the not-given, nor between the world of being and the world of value, but across all the regions between You and It: between presence and object.[8]

*

The present—not that which is like a point and merely designates whatever our thoughts may posit as the end of "elapsed" time, the fiction of the fixed lapse, but the actual and fulfilled present—exists only insofar as presentness, encounter, and relation exist. Only as the You becomes present does presence come into being.

The I of the basic word I-It, the I that is not bodily confronted by a You[9] but surrounded by a multitude of "contents," has only a past and no present. In other words: insofar as a human being makes do with the things that he experiences and uses, he lives in the past, and his moment

[8] *Gegenwart und Gegenstand:* this contrast is developed and echoed in the following sections. The words are discussed on p. 45: *Gegenwart* means both presence and the present as opposed to past and future; and in the next sentence it has been translated "the present."
[9] See note 1 on page 58.

has no presence. He has nothing but objects; but objects consist in having been.

Presence is not what is evanescent and passes but what confronts us, waiting and enduring.[1] And the object is not duration but standing still, ceasing, breaking off, becoming rigid, standing out, the lack of relation, the lack of presence.

What is essential is lived in the present, objects[2] in the past.

*

This essential twofoldness cannot be overcome by in-

[1] *Gegenwart ist . . . das Gegenwartende und Gegenwährende.* The first word is the usual term for the present or presence, the other two capitalized words are coinages and represent plays on the first word.

[2] *Wesenheiten werden in der Gegenwart gelebt, Gegenständlichkeiten in der Vergangenheit.* This is an extraordinary sentence. Both *Wesenheit* and *Gegenständlichkeit* are rare words with no very precise meaning: the effect of the suffixes (*heit* and *keit*) is to add a note of abstractness and generality, comparable to "essencehood" and "objecthood." Using these two words in the plural is most unusual, and saying that the former is lived in the present and the latter in the past is a *tour de force.* In German, as in English, only life can "be lived." Had Buber said *erlebt* (experienced in a living or vital manner), the sentence would be much less puzzling; but in this book he treats experience (*Erfahrung*) as a corollary of object and It, and generally he does not exempt *Erlebnis* which, though more vital and intense, suggests an aesthetic orientation. The last half of the sentence is much less difficult than the first. We have been prepared for it by the two preceding paragraphs; e.g., "objects consist in having been." Whatever is not present to me and—to use my own expression—addressing me as a person, whatever is remembered, discussed, or analyzed, has lapsed into the past and is an object. "Beings are lived in the present" does not make much sense of the first six words, although *Wesen* in this book means being or nature more often than it means essence. Beings simply are not lived; they live, they may address us and change our lives, but to say that they are lived is not merely a solecism but contrary to what Buber says in this book. "What is essential is lived in the present" is linguistically not so outrageous, is much more meaningful, and suggests an idea that is in keeping with the central motifs of the book.

voking a "world of ideas" as a third element that might transcend this opposition. For I speak only of the actual human being, of you and me, of our life and our world, not of any I-in-itself and not of any Being-in-itself. But for an actual human being the real boundary also runs across the world of ideas.

To be sure, some men who in the world of things make do with experiencing and using have constructed for themselves an idea annex or superstructure in which they find refuge and reassurance in the face of intimations of nothingness. At the threshold they take off the clothes of the ugly weekday, shroud themselves in clean garments, and feel restored as they contemplate primal being or what ought to be—something in which their life has no share. It may also make them feel good to proclaim it.

But the It-humanity that some imagine, postulate, and advertise has nothing in common with the bodily humanity to which a human being can truly say You. The noblest fiction is a fetish, the most sublime fictitious senti-ment is a vice. The ideas are just as little enthroned above our heads as they reside inside them; they walk among us and step up to us. Pitiful are those who leave the basic word unspoken, but wretched are those who instead of that ad-dress the ideas with a concept or a slogan as if that were their name!

*

That direct relationships involve some action on[3] what confronts us becomes clear in one of three examples. The essential deed of art determines the process whereby the form becomes a work. That which confronts me is fulfilled through the encounter through which it enters into the world of things in order to remain incessantly effective,

[3] *ein Wirken am:* an odd locution.

incessantly It—but also infinitely able to become again a
You, enchanting and inspiring. It becomes "incarnate":
out of the flood of spaceless and timeless presence it rises
to the shore of continued existence.[4]

Less clear is the element of action in the relation to a
human You. The essential act that here establishes directness is usually understood as a feeling, and thus misunderstood. Feelings accompany the metaphysical and
metapsychical fact of love, but they do not constitute it;
and the feelings that accompany it can be very different.
Jesus' feeling for the possessed man is different from his
feeling for the beloved disciple; but the love is one. Feelings one "has"; love occurs. Feelings dwell in man, but
man dwells in his love. This is no metaphor but actuality:
love does not cling to an I, as if the You were merely its
"content" or object; it is between I and You. Whoever does
not know this, know this with his being, does not know
love, even if he should ascribe to it the feelings that he lives
through,[5] experiences, enjoys, and expresses. Love is a
cosmic force.[6] For those who stand in it and behold in it,
men emerge from their entanglement in busy-ness; [7] and
the good and the evil, the clever and the foolish, the beautiful and the ugly, one after another become actual and a You
for them; that is, liberated, emerging into a unique confrontation.[8] Exclusiveness comes into being miraculously
again and again—and now one can act, help, heal, educate,
raise, redeem. Love is responsibility of an I for a You: in
this consists what cannot consist in any feeling—the equality of all lovers, from the smallest to the greatest and from
the blissfully secure whose life is circumscribed by the life

[4] *das Ufer des Bestands:* see page 53, note 2.
[5] *erlebt.*
[6] *Liebe ist ein welthaftes Wirken.*
[7] *Getriebe.*
[8] *herausgetreten, einzig und gegenüber wesend.*

of one beloved human being to him that is nailed his life
long to the cross of the world, capable of what is immense
and bold enough to risk it: to love *man.*[9]

Let the meaning of action in the third example, that of
the creature and its contemplation, remain mysterious.
Believe in the simple magic of life, in service in the universe, and it will dawn on you what this waiting, peering,
"stretching of the neck"[1] of the creature means. Every
word must falsify; but look, these beings live around you,
and no matter which one you approach you always reach
Being.[2]

*

Relation is reciprocity. My You acts on me as I act on
it. Our students teach us, our works form us. The
"wicked" become a revelation when they are touched by
the sacred basic word. How are we educated by children,
by animals! Inscrutably involved, we live in the currents of
universal reciprocity.

*

—You speak of love as if it were the only relationship
between men; but are you even justified in choosing it as
an example, seeing that there is also hatred?

—As long as love is "blind"—that is, as long as it does
not see a *whole* being—it does not yet truly stand under the

[9] *die Menschen zu lieben.*
[1] Since 1957: "stretching the head forward." Surely, we are to think of
a cat: see pp. 144 ff.
[2] *die Wesen leben um dich herum . . . du kommst immer zum Wesen.* In
another context many translators would, no doubt, render *die Wesen* by
"the creatures" and *zum Wesen* by "the essence." That way something
important would be lost, but these meanings are present.

basic word of relation. Hatred remains blind by its very
nature; one can hate only part of a being. Whoever sees a
whole being and must reject it, is no longer in the dominion of hatred but in the human limitation of the capacity
to say You. It does happen to men that a human being
confronts them and they are unable to address him with
the basic word that always involves an affirmation of
the being one addresses, and then they have to reject
either the other person or themselves: when entering-
into-relationship comes to this barrier, it recognizes its
own relativity which disappears only when this barrier is
removed.

Yet whoever hates directly is closer to a relation than
those who are without love and hate.

*

This, however, is the sublime melancholy of our lot that
every You must become an It in our world. However
exclusively present it may have been in the direct relationship—as soon as the relationship has run its course or is
permeated by *means*,[3] the You becomes an object among
objects, possibly the noblest one and yet one of them,
assigned its measure and boundary. The actualization of
the work involves a loss of actuality. Genuine contemplation never lasts long; the natural being that only now revealed itself to me in the mystery of reciprocity has again
become describable, analyzable, classifiable—the point at
which manifold systems of laws intersect. And even love

[3] *Mittel.* The word translated as "direct" and "directly" in the immediately preceding lines is *unmittelbar.* Even if that were rendered as
"immediate(ly)"—at the cost of giving the impression that Buber speaks
of those who hate right away, instantly—"means" would then have to
be circumscribed by "that which mediates." Cf. p. 62, note 7.

cannot persist in direct relation; it endures, but only in the
alternation of actuality and latency. The human being who
but now was unique and devoid of qualities, not at hand[4]
but only present, not experienceable, only touchable,[5] has
again become a He or She, an aggregate of qualities, a
quantum with a shape.[6] Now I can again abstract from him
the color of his hair, of his speech, of his graciousness; but
as long as I can do that he is my You no longer and not
yet again.

Every You in the world is doomed by its nature to
become a thing or at least to enter into thinghood again
and again. In the language of objects: every thing in the
world can—either before or after it becomes a thing—
appear to some I as its You. But the language of objects
catches only one corner of actual life.

The It is the chrysalis, the You the butterfly.[7] Only it is
not always as if these states took turns so neatly; often it
is an intricately entangled series of events that is tortuously
dual.

*

In the beginning is the relation.

Consider the language of "primitive" peoples, meaning
those who have remained poor in objects and whose life
develops in a small sphere of acts that have a strong presence.[8] The nuclei of this language, their sentence-words—
primal pre-grammatical forms that eventually split into the
multiplicity of different kinds of words—generally designate the wholeness of a relation. We say, "far away"; the

[4] *vorhanden.*
[5] Before 1957: fulfillable.
[6] *ein figurhaftes Quantum.*
[7] Before 1957: eternal chrysalis, . . . eternal butterfly.
[8] *gegenwartsstarker Akte.*

Zulu has a sentence-word instead that means: "where one cries, 'mother, I am lost.'" And the Fuegian surpasses our analytical wisdom with a sentence-word of seven syllables that literally means: "they look at each other, each waiting for the other to offer to do that which both desire but neither wishes to do." In this wholeness persons are still embedded like reliefs without achieving the fully rounded independence of nouns or pronouns. What counts is not these products of analysis and reflection[9] but the genuine original unity, the lived relationship.

We greet those we encounter by wishing them well or by assuring them of our devotion or by commending them to God. But how indirect are these worn-out formulas ("Hail!"[1] no longer suggests anything of the original bestowal of power) compared with the eternally young, physical, relational greeting of the Kaffir, "I see you!" or its American variant, the laughable but sublime "Smell me!"

We may suppose that relations[2] and concepts, as well as the notions of persons and things, have gradually crystallized out of notions of relational processes and states. The elementary, spirit-awakening impressions and stimulations of the "natural man" are derived from relational processes—the living sense of a confrontation—and from relational states—living with one who confronts him. About the moon which he sees every night he does not think much until it approaches him bodily, in his sleep or even while he is awake, and casts a spell over him with its gestures or, touching him, does something wicked or

[9] *Zerlegung und Überlegung.*
[1] *Heil!* Toward the end of the year in which *Ich und Du* was published, Hitler made his abortive putsch in Munich; ten years later *Heil!* and *Heil Hitler!* attained official status in Germany as *der deutsche Gruss,* the German greeting.
[2] Before 1957: designations (*Bezeichnungen* instead of *Beziehungen*).

sweet to him. What he retains is not the visual notion of
the migratory disk of light nor that of a demonic being that
somehow belongs to it, but at first only an image of the
moon's action that surges through his body as a motor
stimulus; and the personal image of an active moon crystallizes only very gradually. Only then is the memory of that
which was unconsciously absorbed every night kindled
into the notion of an agent behind this action. Only then
does it become possible for the You that originally could
not be an object of experience, being simply endured, to
be reified and become a He or She.

The originally relational character of the appearance of
all beings persists and remains effective for a long time.
This may help us to understand a spiritual element of
primitive life that has been discussed a great deal in recent
literature without having been adequately interpreted: that
mysterious power whose concept has been found with all
sorts of variations in the faith and science (both are still one
at this point) of many primitive peoples—that *mana* or
orenda from which we can trace a path all the way to the
original significance of Brahman and even to the *dynamis*
and *charis* of the magical papyruses and the Apostolic letters.[3] It has been designated as a supra-sensible or supernatural force, in terms of our categories which do not do
justice to those of primitive man. The boundaries of his
world are drawn by his bodily experiences to which the
visits of the dead belong quite "naturally." Any assump-
tion that the non-sensible exists must strike him as nonsense. The appearances to which he attributes a "mystical
potency" are all the elementary relational processes—that
is, all the processes about which he thinks at all because
they stimulate his body and leave an impression of such

[3]In the original the passage from the beginning of the paragraph to this
point forms a single sentence.

stimulation in him. The moon and the dead who haunt him at night with pain or lust have this potency; but so do the sun that burns him, the beast that howls at him, the chief whose glance compels him, and the shaman whose song fills him with strength for the hunt. *Mana* is that which is active and effective,[4] that which has made the moon person up there in the sky a blood-curdling You, that of which a memory trace remained when the impression of a stimulus turned into the impression of an object, although *mana* itself always appears only in an agent. It is that with which we ourselves, if we possess it—say, in a miracle stone—can bring about similar effects. The primitive "world" is magical not because any human power of magic might be at its center, but rather because any such human power is only a variant of the general power that is the source of all effective action.[5] The causality of his world is not a continuum; it is a force that flashes, strikes, and is effective ever again like lightning, a volcanic motion without continuity. *Mana* is a primitive abstraction, probably more primitive than numbers, for example, but no more supernatural. Memory, educating itself, constructs a series of the major relational events and the elementary upheavals. What is most important for the drive for preservation and most noteworthy for the drive for knowledge, namely, that which is active and effective,[6] stands out most clearly and gains independence, while the less important, that which is not shared, the changeful You of the experiences, recedes, remains isolated in man's memory, gradually becomes an object and even more gradually gets arranged in groups and species. But the third element, gruesomely detached and at times spookier than the dead and the

[4] *Mana ist eben das Wirkende . . .*
[5] *der alle wesentliche Wirkung entstammt.*
[6] *eben das "Wirkende" . . .*

moon, becomes more and more inexorably clear until finally the other partner that always remains the same emerges: "I."

The original drive for "self"-preservation is no more accompanied by any I-consciousness than any other drive. What wants to propagate itself is not the I but the body that does not yet know of any I.[7] Not the I but the body wants to make things, tools, toys, wants to be "inventive."[8] And even in the primitive function of cognition one cannot find any *cognosco ergo sum*[9] of even the most naïve kind, nor any conception, however childlike, of an experiencing subject. Only when the primal encounters,[1] the vital primal words I-acting-You[2] and You-acting-I, have been split and the participle has been reified and hypostatized, does the I emerge with the force of an element.

*

In the history of the primitive mind[3] the fundamental difference between the two basic words appears in this: even in the original relational event, the primitive man speaks the basic word I-You in a natural, as it were still unformed manner, not yet having recognized himself as an I; but the basic word I-It is made possible only by this recognition, by the detachment of the I.

[7] Cf. the chapter "On the Despisers of the Body" in Part One of Nietzsche's *Zarathustra*, which the young Buber translated into Polish: " 'I,' you say . . . But greater is . . . your body and its great reason: that does not say 'I,' but does 'I.' "
[8] *Urheber*
[9] I know, therefore I am.
[1] *Urerlebnisse.*
[2] *Ich-wirkend-Du* is as odd as the translation above.
[3] *in der Geistesgeschichte des Primitiven.*

The former word splits into I and You, but it did not originate as their aggregate, it antedates any I. The latter originated as an aggregate of I and It, it postdates the I.

Owing to its exclusiveness, the primitive relational event includes the I. For by its nature this event contains only two partners, man and what confronts him, both in their full actuality, and the world becomes a dual system; and thus man begins to have some sense of that cosmic pathos[4] of the I without as yet realizing this.

In the natural fact, on the other hand, that will give way to the basic word I-It and I-related experience, the I is not yet included. This fact is the discreteness of the human body as the carrier of its sensations, from its environment. In this particularity the body learns to know and discriminate itself, but this discrimination remains on the plane where things are next to each other, and therefore it cannot assume the character of implicit I-likeness.[5]

But once the I of the relation has emerged and has become existent in its detachment, it somehow etherializes and functionalizes itself[6] and enters into the natural fact of the discreteness of the body from its environment, awakening I-likeness in it. Only now can the conscious I-act, the first form of the basic word I-It, of experience by an I, come into being. The I that has emerged proclaims itself as the carrier of sensations and the environment as their object. Of course, this happens in a "primitive" and not in an "epistemological" manner; yet once the sentence "I see the tree" has been pronounced in such a way that it no longer relates a relation between a human I and a tree You but the perception of the tree object by the human consciousness, it has erected the crucial barrier between sub-

[4] *Pathetik.*
[5] *Ichhaftigkeit.*
[6] *sich seltsam verdünnend und funktionalisierend.*

ject and object; the basic word I-It, the word of separation, has been spoken.

*

—Then our melancholy lot took shape in primal history?

—Indeed, it developed—insofar as man's conscious life developed in primal history. But in conscious life cosmic being recurs as human becoming. Spirit appears in time as a product, even a byproduct, of nature, and yet it is spirit that envelops nature timelessly.

The opposition of the two basic words has many names in the ages and worlds; but in its nameless truth it inheres in the creation.

*

—Then you believe after all in some paradise in the primal age of humanity?

—Even if it was a hell—and the age to which we can go back in historical thought was certainly full of wrath and dread and torment and cruelty—unreal it was not.

Primal man's experiences of encounter were scarcely a matter of tame delight; but even violence against a being one really confronts[7] is better than ghostly solicitude for faceless digits! From the former a path leads to God, from the latter only to nothingness.[8]

*

[7] *Gewalt am real erlebten Wesen.*
[8] *ins Nichts.*

Even if we could fully understand the life of the primitive, it would be no more than a metaphor for that of the truly primal man. Hence the primitive affords us only brief glimpses into the temporal sequence of the two basic words. More complete information we receive from the child.

Here it becomes unmistakably clear how the spiritual reality of the basic words emerges from a natural[9] reality: that of the basic word I-You from a natural association,[1] that of the basic word I-It from a natural discreteness.

The prenatal life of the child is a pure natural association, a flowing toward each other, a bodily reciprocity; and the life horizon of the developing being appears uniquely inscribed, and yet also not inscribed, in that of the being that carries it; for the womb in which it dwells is not solely that of the human mother. This association is so cosmic that it seems like the imperfect deciphering of a primeval inscription when we are told in the language of Jewish myth that in his mother's womb man knows the universe and forgets it at birth. And as the secret image of a wish, this association remains to us. But this longing ought not to be taken for a craving to go back, as those suppose who consider the spirit, which they confound with their own intellect, a parasite of nature. For the spirit is nature's blossom, albeit exposed to many diseases. What this longing aims for is the cosmic association of the being that has burst into spirit with its true You.

Every developing human child rests, like all developing beings, in the womb of the great mother—the undifferentiated, not yet formed primal world. From this it detaches itself to enter a personal life, and it is only in dark hours

[9] naturhaften.
[1] naturhaften Verbundenheit. "Association" is used in this book only to render Verbundenheit.

when we slip out of this again (as happens even to the healthy, night after night) that we are close to her again. But this detachment is not sudden and catastrophic like that from the bodily mother. The human child is granted some time to exchange the natural association with the world that is slipping away for a spiritual association—a relationship. From the glowing darkness of the chaos he has stepped into the cool and light creation without immediately possessing it: he has to get it up, as it were, and make it a reality for himself; he gains his world by seeing, listening, feeling, forming.[2] It is in encounter that the creation reveals its formhood;[3] it does not pour itself into senses that are waiting but deigns to meet those that are reaching out. What is to surround the finished human being as an object, has to be acquired and wooed strenuously by him while he is still developing.[4] No thing is a component of experience or reveals itself except through the reciprocal force of confrontation. Like primitives, the child lives between sleep and sleep (and a large part of waking is still sleep), in the lightning and counter-lightning of encounter.

The innateness of the longing for relation is apparent even in the earliest and dimmest stage. Before any particulars can be perceived, dull glances push into the unclear space toward the indefinite; and at times when there is obviously no desire for nourishment, soft projections of the hands reach, aimlessly to all appearances, into the empty air toward the indefinite.[5] Let anyone call this animalic:

[2] *es muss sich seine Welt erschauen, erhorchen, ertasten, erbilden.* Cf. p. 55, note 4 on *erfahren.*
[3] *Gestaltigkeit* is a coinage.
[4] *Was den fertigen Menschen ... umspielen wird, muss vom entstehenden in angestrengter Handlung erworben, umworben werden.*
[5] *und ... allem Anschein nach zwecklos suchen, greifen die weichen Handentwürfe in die leere Luft ...* The word order and the choice of words are most unusual.

that does not help our comprehension. For precisely these glances will eventually, after many trials, come to rest upon a red wallpaper arabesque and not leave it until the soul of red has opened up to them. Precisely this motion will gain its sensuous form and definiteness in contact with a shaggy toy bear and eventually apprehend lovingly and unforgettably a complete body: in both cases not experience of an object but coming to grips with a living, active being that confronts us, if only in our "imagination." (But this "imagination" is by no means a form of "panpsychism"; it is the drive to turn everything into a You, the drive to pan-relation—and where it does not find a living, active being that confronts it but only an image or symbol of that, it supplies the living activity from its own fullness.) Little inarticulate sounds still ring out senselessly and persistently into the nothing; but one day they will have turned imperceptibly into a conversation—with what? Perhaps with a bubbling tea kettle, but into a conversation. Many a motion that is called a reflex is a sturdy trowel for the person building up his world. It is not as if a child first saw an object and then entered into some relationship with that. Rather, the longing for relation is primary, the cupped hand into which the being that confronts us nestles; and the relation to that, which is a wordless anticipation of saying You, comes second. But the genesis of the thing is a late product that develops out of the split of the primal encounters,[6] out of the separation of the associated partners—as does the genesis of the I. In the beginning is the relation—as the category of being, as readiness, as a form that reaches out to be filled, as a model of the soul; the *a priori* of relation; *the innate You.*

In the relationships through which we live, the innate You is realized in the You we encounter: that this, com-

[6] *Urerlebnisse.*

prehended as a being we confront[7] and accepted as exclusive, can finally be addressed with the basic word, has its ground in the *a priori* of relation.

In the drive for contact (originally, a drive for tactile contact, then also for optical contact with another being) the innate You comes to the fore quite soon, and it becomes ever clearer that the drive aims at reciprocity, at "tenderness." But it also determines the inventive drive[8] which emerges later (the drive to produce things synthetically or, where that is not possible, analytically—through taking or tearing apart), and thus the product is "personified" and a "conversation" begins. The development of the child's soul is connected indissolubly with his craving for the You, with the fulfillments[9] and disappointments of this craving, with the play of his experiments and his tragic seriousness when he feels at a total loss. Any real understanding of these phenomena is compromised by all attempts to reduce them to narrower spheres and can be promoted only when in contemplating and discussing them we recall their cosmic-metacosmic origin. We must remember the reach beyond that undifferentiated, not yet formed[1] primal world from which the corporeal[2] individual that was born into the world has emerged completely, but not yet the bodily,[3] the actualized being that has to evolve from it gradually through entering into relationships.

*

[7] *Die erlebten Beziehungen sind Realisierungen des eingeborenen Du am begegnenden; dass dieses als Gegenüber gefasst . . .*
[8] *Urbebertrieb.* Cf. p. 73, note 8 and the preceding text.
[9] Until 1957: Satisfactions.
[1] *vorgestaltigen.* This is a coinage. See p. 77, note 3.
[2] *körperliche.*
[3] *leibliche:* In ordinary German *körperlich* and *leiblich* are synonyms.

Man becomes an I through a You. What confronts us comes and vanishes, relational events take shape and scatter, and through these changes crystallizes, more and more each time, the consciousness of the constant partner, the I-consciousness. To be sure, for a long time it appears only woven into the relation to a You, discernible as that which reaches for but is not a You; but it comes closer and closer to the bursting point until one day the bonds are broken and the I confronts its detached self for a moment like a You—and then it takes possession of itself and henceforth enters into relations in full consciousness.

Only now can the other basic word be put together. For although the You of the relation always paled again, it never became the It of an I—an object of detached perception and experience, which is what it will become henceforth—but as it were an It for itself, something previously unnoticed that was waiting for the new relational event. Of course, the maturing body[4] as the carrier of its sensations and the executor of its drives stood out from its environment, but only in the next-to-each-other where one finds one's way, not yet in the absolute separation of I and object. Now, however, the detached I is transformed—reduced from substantial fullness to the functional one-dimensionality[5] of a subject that experiences and uses objects—and thus approaches all the "It for itself," overpowers it and joins with it to form the other basic word. The man who has acquired an I[6] and says I-It assumes a position before things but does not confront them in the current of reciprocity. He bends down to examine particulars under the objectifying magnifying glass of close scrutiny, or he uses the objectifying telescope of

[4] *der zum Leib reifende Körper:* see the two preceding notes.
[5] *Punkthaftigkeit:* a coinage meaning pointlikeness.
[6] *Der ichhaft gewordene Mensch.*

distant vision to arrange them as mere scenery. In his contemplation he isolates them without any feeling for the exclusive or joins them without any world feeling. The former could be attained only through relation, and the latter only by starting from that. Only now he experiences things as aggregates of qualities. Qualities, to be sure, had remained in his memory after every encounter,[7] as belonging to the remembered You; but only now things seem to him to be constructed of their qualities. Only by drawing on his memory of the relation—dreamlike, visual, or conceptual, depending on the kind of man he is—he supplements the core that revealed itself powerfully in the You, embracing all qualities: the substance. Only now does he place things in a spatio-temporal-causal context; only now does each receive its place, its course, its measurability, its conditionality. The You also appears in space, but only in an exclusive confrontation in which everything else can only be background from which it emerges, not its boundary and measure. The You appears in time, but in that of a process that is fulfilled in itself—a process lived through not as a piece that is a part of a constant and organized sequence but in a "duration"[8] whose purely intensive dimension can be determined only by starting from the You. It appears simultaneously as acting on and as acted upon,[9] but not as if it had been fitted into a causal chain; rather as, in its reciprocity with the I, the beginning and end of the event. This is part of the basic truth of the human world: only It can be put in order. Only as things cease to be our You and become our It do they become subject to coordination. The You knows no system of coordinates.

[7] *Beziehungserlebnis:* literally, living experience of relation.
[8] Buber in March 1937: What is meant is Bergson's *durée.*
[9] *als Wirkung und als Wirkung empfangend.*

But having got this far, we must also make another pro-
nouncement without which this piece of the basic truth
would remain an unfit fragment: an ordered world is not
the world order. There are moments of the secret ground
in which world order is beheld as present. Then the tone
is heard all of a sudden whose uninterpretable score the
ordered world is. These moments are immortal; none are
more evanescent. They leave no content that could be
preserved, but their force enters into the creation and
into man's knowledge, and the radiation of its force penetrates the ordered world and thaws it again and again.
Thus the history of the individual, thus the history of the
race.

*

The world is twofold for man in accordance with his
twofold attitude.

He perceives the being that surrounds him, plain things
and beings as things; he perceives what happens around
him, plain processes and actions as processes, things that
consist of qualities and processes that consist of moments,
things recorded in terms of spatial coordinates and processes recorded in terms of temporal coordinates, things
and processes that are bounded by other things and processes and capable of being measured against and compared with those others—an ordered world, a detached
world. This world is somewhat reliable; it has density and
duration; its articulation can be surveyed; one can get it out
again and again; one recounts it with one's eyes closed and
then checks with one's eyes open. There it stands—right
next to your skin if you think of it that way, or nestled in
your soul if you prefer that: it is your object and remains

that, according to your pleasure—and remains primally alien both outside and inside you. You perceive it and take it for your "truth";[1] it permits itself to be taken by you, but it does not give itself to you. It is only *about* it that you can come to an understanding with others; although it takes a somewhat different form for everybody, it is prepared to be a common object for you; but you cannot encounter others in it. Without it you cannot remain alive; its reliability preserves you; but if you were to die into it, then you would be buried in nothingness.

Or man encounters being and becoming as what confronts him—always only *one* being and every thing only as a being. What is there reveals itself to him in the occurrence, and what occurs there happens to him as being. Nothing else is present but this one, but this one cosmically.[2] Measure and comparison have fled. It is up to you how much of the immeasurable becomes reality for you. The encounters do not order themselves to become a world, but each is for you a sign of the world order. They have no association with each other, but every one guarantees your association with the world. The world that appears to you in this way is unreliable, for it appears always new to you, and you cannot take it by its word. It lacks density, for everything in it permeates everything else. It lacks duration, for it comes even when not called and vanishes even when you cling to it. It cannot be surveyed: if you try to make it surveyable, you lose it. It comes— comes to fetch you—and if it does not reach you or encounter you it vanishes, but it comes again, transformed. It does not stand outside you, it touches your ground; and

---

[1] *Du nimmst sie wahr, nimmst sie dir zur "Wahrheit"* . . . This is a gloss on the literal meaning of the German verb *wahrnehmen* which is the ordinary word for perceive.
[2] *aber dies eine welthaft.*

if you say "soul of my soul" you have not said too much.
But beware of trying to transpose it into your soul—that
way you destroy it. It is your present; you have a present
only insofar as you have it;[3] and you can make it into an
object for you and experience and use it—you must do that
again and again—and then you have no present any more.
Between you and it there is a reciprocity of giving: you say
You to it and give yourself to it; it says You to you and
gives itself to you. You cannot come to an understanding
about it with others; you are lonely with it; but it teaches
you to encounter others and to stand your ground in such
encounters; and through the grace of its advents and the
melancholy of its departures it leads you to that You in
which the lines of relation, though parallel, intersect. It
does not help you to survive; it only helps you to have
intimations of eternity.

The It-world hangs together in space and time.

The You-world does not hang together in space and
time.

The individual You *must* become an It when the event
of relation has run its course.

The individual It *can* become a You by entering into the
event of relation.

These are the two basic privileges of the It-world. They
induce man to consider the It-world as the world in which
one has to live and also can live comfortably—and that
even offers us all sorts of stimulations and excitements,
activities and knowledge. In this firm and wholesome
chronicle the You-moments appear as queer lyric-dramatic
episodes. Their spell may be seductive, but they pull us
dangerously to extremes, loosening the well-tried structure, leaving behind more doubt than satisfaction, shaking
up our security—altogether uncanny, altogether indis-

[3]In 1957 Buber changed the German word order. Cf. p. 63, note 8.

pensable.[4] Since one must after all return into "the world," why not stay in it in the first place? Why not call to order that which confronts us and send it home into objectivity? And when one cannot get around saying You, perhaps to one's father, wife, companion—why not say You and mean It? After all, producing the sound "You" with one's vocal cords does not by any means entail speaking the uncanny basic word. Even whispering an amorous You with one's soul is hardly dangerous as long as in all seriousness one means nothing but experiencing and using.

One cannot live in the pure present: it would consume us if care were not taken that it is overcome quickly and thoroughly. But in pure past one can live; in fact, only there can a life be arranged. One only has to fill every moment with experiencing and using, and it ceases to burn.

And in all the seriousness of truth, listen:[5] without It a human being cannot live. But whoever lives only with that is not human.[6]

[4] Until 1957: dispensable. At first glance it might seem as if Buber had changed his mind. But "dispensable" was obviously meant ironically, like the rest of the passage, and actually was much more consistent with the immediately following sentence. Eventually Buber evidently felt dissatisfied with his sustained irony and decided to bring the reader up short with a sudden show of his real hand. But "indispensable" does not only break the mood; it is flatly contradicted by the following sentences. The first translator of the book took no note of this change—or a great many others—in his "Second Edition." In this case, I think Buber's change is for the worse.

[5] Buber does not say "listen" but *du*. Here "you" would be rather unidiomatic and unnatural, but in German lovers and close friends sometimes use *du* in this way as an expression of intimacy.

[6] Cf. Hillel's words: "If I am not for myself, who will be? And if I am only for myself, what am I? And if not now, when?" (Avoth I: 14).

Second Part

HOWEVER THE HISTORY of the individual and that of the human race may diverge in other respects, they agree in this at least: both signify a progressive increase of the It-world.

Regarding the history of the race this is often doubted. People point out that successive cultures begin with a primitive stage that is colored differently but always has essentially the same structure, involving a small world of objects; and thus it is the life of each individual culture and not that of the race that is held to correspond to the life of the individual.[1] But if we disregard those cultures that seem to be isolated, we find that those that are under the historical influence of others take over their It-world at a certain stage that is not so early but precedes the great age —sometimes by immediately accepting it from a culture that is still contemporary, as did the Greeks from the Egyptians; at other times indirectly from a past culture, as Occidental Christendom accepted the Greek It-world. They enlarge their It-world not only through their own experience but also by accepting alien influences, and it is

[1]An allusion to Oswald Spengler whose *Decline of the West* had just appeared and was widely debated.

only then that the It-world which has grown in this way experiences its crucial expansion which involves discovery. (Let us ignore for the moment the overwhelming share in this development of the vision and deeds of the You-world.) Generally, the It-world of every culture is therefore more comprehensive than that of its predecessors, and in spite of some stoppages and apparent regressions the progressive increase of the It-world is clearly discernible in history. It is not essential in this connection whether the "world" of a culture should be characterized more as finite or whether we should attribute to it so-called infinity or, more correctly speaking, non-finitude: a "finite" world may very well contain more components, things, and processes than an "infinite" one. It should also be noted that we must compare not only the extent of their knowledge of nature but also that of their social differentiation and their technical achievements because both expand the world of objects.

The basic relation of man to the It-world includes experience, which constitutes this world ever again, and use, which leads it toward its multifarious purpose—the preservation, alleviation, and equipment of human life. With the extent of the It-world the capacity for experiencing and using it must also increase. To be sure, the individual can replace direct experience more and more with indirect experience, the "acquisition of information"; and he can abbreviate use more and more until it becomes specialized "utilization": a continual improvement of capacity from generation to generation is nevertheless indispensable. This is what is usually meant when people speak of a progressive development of the life of the spirit. This certainly involves the real linguistic sin against the spirit; for this "life of the spirit" is usually the obstacle that keeps man from living in the spirit, and at best it is only the matter that has to be mastered and formed before it can be incorporated. The obstacle: for the improvement of the capacity for experience and use generally involves a decrease in man's power to relate—that power which alone can enable man to live in the spirit.

*

Spirit in its human manifestation is man's response to his You. Man speaks in many tongues—tongues of language, of art, of action—but the spirit is one; it is response to the You that appears from the mystery and addresses us from the mystery. Spirit is word. And even as verbal speech may first become word in the brain of man and then become sound in his throat, although both are merely refractions of the true event because in truth language does not reside in man but man stands in language and speaks out of it—so it is with all words, all spirit. Spirit is not in the I but between I and You. It is not like the blood that circulates in you but like the air in which you breathe. Man lives in the spirit when he is able to respond to his You. He is able to do that when he enters into this relation with his whole being. It is solely by virtue of his power to relate that man is able to live in the spirit.

But it is here that the fate[2] of the relational event rears up most powerfully. The more powerful the response, the more powerfully it ties down the You and as by a spell binds it into an object. Only silence toward the You, the silence of *all* tongues, the taciturn waiting in the unformed, undifferentiated, prelinguistic word leaves the You free and stands together with it in reserve where the spirit does not manifest itself but is. All response binds the You into the It-world. That is the melancholy of man, and

[2] *Schicksal.*

that is his greatness. For thus knowledge, thus works, thus image and example come into being among the living.

But whatever has thus been changed into It and frozen into a thing among things is still endowed with the meaning and the destiny[3] to change back ever again. Ever again —that was the intention in that hour of the spirit when it bestowed itself upon man and begot the response in him —the object shall catch fire and become present, returning to the element from which it issued, to be beheld and lived by men as present.

The fulfillment of this meaning and this destiny is frustrated by the man who has become reconciled to the It-world as something that is to be experienced and used and who holds down what is tied into it instead of freeing it, who observes it instead of heeding it,[4] and instead of receiving it utilizes it.

Knowledge: as he beholds what confronts him, its being is disclosed to the knower. What he beheld as present he will have to comprehend as an object, compare with objects, assign a place in an order of objects, and describe and analyze objectively; only as an It can it be absorbed into the store of knowledge. But in the act of beholding it was no thing among things, no event among events; it was present exclusively. It is not in the law that is afterward derived from the appearance but in the appearance itself that the being communicates itself. That we think the universal is merely an unreeling of the skeinlike event that was beheld in the particular, in a confrontation. And now it is locked into the It-form of conceptual knowledge. Whoever unlocks it and beholds it again as present, fulfills the meaning

---

[3] *Bestimmung.*
[4] *statt ihm zuzublicken:* in German one can *zuhören* (listen; literally: hear to) but hardly *zublicken.* The point here is not to observe a direct object but to respond to a You.

of that act of knowledge as something that is actual and active between men. But knowledge can also be pursued by stating: "so that is how matters stand; that is the name of the thing; that is how it is constituted; that is where it belongs." What has become an It is then taken as an It, experienced and used as an It, employed along with other things for the project of finding one's way in the world, and eventually for the project of "conquering" the world.

Art, too: as he beholds what confronts him, the form discloses itself to the artist. He conjures it into an image. The image does not stand in a world of gods but in this great world of men. Of course, it is "there" even when no human eye afflicts it; but it sleeps. The Chinese poet relates that men did not want to hear the song that he was playing on his flute of jade; then he played it to the gods, and they inclined their ears; and ever since men, too, have listened to the song—and thus he went from the gods to those with whom the image cannot dispense. As in a dream it looks for the encounter with man in order that he may undo the spell and embrace the form for a timeless moment. And there he comes and experiences what there is to be experienced: that is how it is made, or this is what it expresses, or its qualities are such and such, and on top of all that perhaps also how it might rate.

Not that scientific and aesthetic understanding is not necessary—but it should do its work faithfully and immerse itself and disappear in that truth of the relation which surpasses understanding and embraces what is understandable.

And thirdly: that which towers above the spirit of knowledge and the spirit of art because here evanescent, corporeal man need not banish himself into the enduring matter but outlasts it and rises, himself an image, on the starry sky of the spirit, as the music of his living speech roars around him—pure action, the act that is not arbitrary. Here the You appeared to man out of a deeper mystery, addressed him out of the dark, and he responded with his life. Here the word has become life, and this life, whether it fulfilled the law or broke the law—both are required on occasion lest the spirit die on earth—is teaching. Thus it stands before posterity in order to teach it, not what is and not what ought to be, but how one lives in the spirit, in the countenance[5] of the You. And that means: it stands ready to become a You for them at any time, opening up the You-world; no, it does not stand ready, it always comes toward them and touches them. But they, having become uneager and inept for such living intercourse that opens up a world, are well informed; they have imprisoned the person in history, and his speech in a library; they have codified the fulfillment or the breach, it does not matter which; nor are they stingy with reverence and even adoration, adequately mixed with some psychology, as is only proper for modern man. O lonely countenance, starlike in the dark; O living finger upon an insensitive forehead; O steps whose echo is fading away!

*

The improvement of the ability to experience and use generally involves a decrease in man's power to relate.

The man who samples the spirit as if it were spirits[6]— what is he to do with the beings that live around him?

Standing under the basic word of separation which keeps apart I and It, he has divided his life with his fellow men into two neatly defined districts: institutions and feelings. It-district and I-district.

[5] *Angesicht:* the word recurs often in this book. It sounds much more elevated than *Gesicht* (face).
[6] *der den Geist sich zum Genussmittel präparierte.*

Institutions are what is "out there" where for all kinds of purposes one spends time, where one works, negotiates, influences, undertakes, competes, organizes, administers, officiates, preaches; the halfway orderly and on the whole coherent structure where, with the manifold participation of human heads and human limbs, the round of affairs runs its course.

Feelings are what is "in here" where one lives and recovers from the institutions. Here the spectrum of the emotions swings before the interested eye; here one enjoys one's inclination and one's hatred, pleasure and, if it is not too bad, pain. Here one is at home and relaxes in one's rocking chair.

Institutions comprise a complicated forum; feelings, a boudoir that at least provides a good deal of diversity.

This separation, to be sure, is continually endangered, as our sportive feelings break into the most objective institutions; but with a little good will it can always be restored.

A dependable separation is most difficult in the areas of our so-called personal life. In marriage, for example, it is not always so simple to attain; but time works wonders. In the areas of so-called public life it is eminently successful: consider, for example, how in the age of political parties, but also of groups and "movements" that claim to be above parties, heaven-storming congresses alternate flawlessly with the day-to-day operations that crawl along on the ground, whether mechanized and evenly or organically and slovenly.

But the severed It of institutions is a golem,[7] and the severed I of feelings is a fluttering soul-bird.[8] Neither knows the human being; one only the instance and the other one only the "object." Neither knows person or community. Neither knows the present: these, however

[7]Buber's gloss, March 1937: "an animated clod without a soul."
[8]*Ibid.:* An allusion to the "mythical notion of the soul as a bird."

modern, know only the rigid past, that which is finished, while those, however persistent, know only the fleeting moment, that which is not yet. Neither has access to actual life. Institutions yield no public life; feelings, no personal life.

That institutions yield no public life is felt by more and more human beings, to their sorrow: this is the source of the distress and search of our age. That feelings yield no personal life has been recognized by few so far; for they seem to be the home of what is most personal. And once one has learnt, like modern man, to become greatly preoccupied with one's own feelings, even despair over their unreality will not easily open one's eyes; after all, such despair is also a feeling and quite interesting.

Those who suffer because institutions yield no public life have thought of a remedy: feelings are to loosen up or thaw or explode the institutions, as if they could be renewed by feelings, by introducing the "freedom of feelings." When the automatized state yokes together totally uncongenial citizens without creating or promoting any fellowship, it is supposed to be replaced by a loving community. And this loving community is supposed to come into being when people come together, prompted by free, exuberant feeling, and want to live together. But that is not how things are. True community does not come into being because people have feelings for each other (though that is required, too), but rather on two accounts: all of them have to stand in a living, reciprocal relationship to a single living center, and they have to stand in a living, reciprocal relationship to one another. The second event has its source in the first but is not immediately given with it. A living reciprocal relationship includes feelings but is not derived from them. A community is built upon a living, reciprocal relationship, but the builder is the living, active center.

Even institutions of so-called personal life cannot be re-
formed by a free feeling (although this is also required).
Marriage can never be renewed except by that which is
always the source of all true marriage: that two human
beings reveal the You to one another. It is of this that the
You that is I for neither of them builds a marriage. This is
the metaphysical and metapsychical fact of love which is
merely accompanied by feelings of love. Whoever wishes
to renew a marriage on another basis is not essentially
different from those who want to abolish it: both declare
that they no longer know the fact. Indeed, take the much
discussed eroticism of our age and subtract everything that
is really egocentric[9]—in other words, every relationship in
which one is not at all present to the other,[1] but each uses
the other only for self-enjoyment—what would remain?

True public and true personal life are two forms of association. For them to originate and endure, feelings are
required as a changing content, and institutions are required as a constant form; but even the combination of
both still does not create human life which is created only
by a third element: the central presence of the You, or
rather, to speak more truthfully, the central You that is
received in the present.

                              *

The basic word I-It does not come from evil—any more
than matter comes from evil.[2] It comes from evil—like
matter that presumes to be that which has being.[3] When

[9] *was Ichbezogenheit ist.*
[1] *worin eins dem andern gar nicht gegenwärtig, von ihm gar nicht vergegen-
wärtigt wird.*
[2] The phrase harks back to Matthew 5:37.
[3] *das Seiende zu sein.*

man lets it have its way, the relentlessly growing It-world grows over him like weeds, his own I loses its actuality, until the incubus over him and the phantom inside him exchange the whispered confession of their need for redemption.

*

—But isn't the communal life of modern man bound to be submerged in the It-world? Consider the two chambers of this life, the economy and the state: are they even thinkable in their present dimensions and ramifications, except on the basis of a superior renunciation of all "immediacy" —and even an inexorably resolute repudiation of any "alien" authority that does not itself have its source in this area? And if the I that experiences and uses holds sway here—in the economy, the I that uses goods and services; in politics, the I that uses opinions and aspirations—is it not precisely to this absolute dominion that we owe the extensive and firm structure of the great "objective" fabrics in these two spheres? Doesn't the form-giving greatness of leading statesmen and businessmen depend on their way of seeing the human beings with whom they have to deal not as carriers of an inexperienceable You but rather as centers of services and aspirations that have to be calculated and employed according to their specific capacities? Wouldn't their world come crashing down upon them if they refused to add up He + He + He to get an It, and tried instead to determine the sum of You and You and You, which can never be anything else than You? What would this come to if not an exchange of form-giving mastery for a puttering dilettantism, and of lucid, powerful reason for murky enthusiasm? And when we turn our eyes from the leaders to the led and consider the fashion of modern work and possession, don't we find that modern developments have expunged almost every trace of a life in which human beings confront each other and have meaningful relationships? It would be absurd to try to reverse this development; and if one could bring off this absurdity, the tremendous precision instrument of this civilization would be destroyed at the same time, although this alone makes life possible for the tremendously increased numbers of humanity.

—Speaker, you speak too late. But a moment ago you might have believed your own speech; now this is no longer possible. For an instant ago you saw no less than I that the state is no longer led: the stokers still pile up coal, but the leaders merely *seem* to rule the racing engines. And in this instant while you speak, you can hear as well as I how the machinery of the economy is beginning to hum in an unwonted manner; the overseers give you a superior smile, but death lurks in their hearts. They tell you that they have adjusted the apparatus to modern conditions; but you notice that henceforth they can only adjust themselves to the apparatus, as long as that permits it. Their spokesmen instruct you that the economy is taking over the heritage of the state; you know that there is nothing to be inherited but the despotism of the proliferating It under which the I, more and more impotent, is still dreaming that it is in command.

Man's communal life cannot dispense any more than he himself with the It-world—over which the presence of the You floats like the spirit over the face of the waters. Man's will to profit and will to power are natural and legitimate as long as they are tied to the will to human relations and carried by it. There is no evil drive until the drive detaches itself from our being; the drive that is wedded to and

determined by our being[4] is the plasma of communal life,
while the detached drive spells its disintegration. The
economy as the house of the will to profit and the state as
the house of the will to power[5] participate in life as long
as they participate in the spirit. If they abjure the spirit,
they abjure life. To be sure, life takes its time about settling
the score, and for quite a while one may still think that one
sees a form move where for a long time a mere mechanism
has been whirring. Introducing some sort of immediacy at
this point is surely futile. Loosening the framework of the
economy or the state cannot make up for the fact that
neither stands any longer under the supremacy of the You-
saying spirit, and stirring up the periphery cannot replace
the living relationship to the center. The structures of
communal human life derive their life from the fullness of
the relational force that permeates their members, and
they derive their embodied form from the saturation of this
force by the spirit. The statesman or businessman who
serves the spirit is no dilettante. He knows well that he
cannot simply confront the people with whom he has to
deal as so many carriers of the You, without undoing his
own work. Nevertheless he ventures to do this, not simply
but up to the limit suggested to him by the spirit; and the
spirit does suggest a limit to him, and the venture that
would have exploded a severed structure succeeds where
the presence of the You floats above. He does not become
a babbling enthusiast; he serves the truth which, though
supra-rational, does not disown reason but holds it in her
lap. What he does in communal life is no different from
what is done in personal life by a man who knows that he

[4]being, both times: *Wesen;* "our" is not in the original.
[5]*das Gehäuse des Machtwillens.* Buber speaks of *Nutzwillen* and *Macht-
willen* and does not employ the phrase used more often by Nietzsche:
Wille zur Macht.

cannot actualize the You in some pure fashion but who nevertheless bears witness of it daily to the It, defining the limit every day anew, according to the right and measure of that day—discovering the limit anew. Neither work nor possessions can be redeemed on their own but only by starting from the spirit. It is only from the presence of the spirit that significance and joy can flow into all work, and reverence and the strength to sacrifice into all possessions, not to the brim but *quantum satis*—and that all that is worked and possessed, though it remains attached to the It-world, can nevertheless be transfigured to the point where it confronts us and represents the You. There is no back-behind-it; there is, even at the moment of the most profound need—indeed, only then—a previously unsuspected beyond-it.

Whether it is the state that regulates the economy or the economy that directs the state is unimportant as long as both are unchanged. Whether the institutions of the state become freer and those of the economy juster, that is important, but not for the question concerning actual life that is being posed here; for they cannot become free and just on their own. What is decisive is whether the spirit—the You-saying, responding spirit—remains alive and actual; whether what remains of it in communal human life continues to be subjected to the state and the economy or whether it becomes independently active; whether what abides of it in individual human life incorporates itself again in communal life. But that certainly cannot be accomplished by dividing communal life into independent realms that also include "the life of the spirit." That would merely mean that the regions immersed in the It-world would be abandoned forever to this despotism, while the spirit would lose all actuality. For the spirit in itself can never act independently upon life; that it can do only in the world—with its force which penetrates and transforms the It-world. The spirit is truly "at home with itself "[6] when it can confront the world that is opened up to it, give itself to the world, and redeem it and, through the world, also itself. But the spirituality that represents the spirit nowadays is so scattered, weakened, degenerate, and full of contradictions that it could not possibly do this until it had first returned to the essence of the spirit: being able to say You.

*

In the It-world causality holds unlimited sway. Every event that is either perceivable by the senses and "physical" or discovered or found in introspection and "psychological" is considered to be of necessity caused and a cause. Those events which may be regarded as purposive form no exception insofar as they also belong in the continuum of the It-world: this continuum tolerates a teleology, but only as a reversal that is worked into one part of causality without diminishing its complete continuity.

The unlimited sway of causality in the It-world, which is of fundamental importance for the scientific ordering of nature, is not felt to be oppressive by the man who is not confined to the It-world but free to step out of it again and again into the world of relation. Here I and You confront each other freely in a reciprocity that is not involved in or tainted by any causality; here man finds guaranteed the freedom of his being and of being.[7] Only those who know relation and who know of the presence of the You have the capacity for decision. Whoever makes a decision is free

[6] *"bei sich":* this locution and its application to the spirit are Hegelian. Cf. *an sich* (in itself) above, where it is contrasted with *an der Welt* (in the world).
[7] *die Freibeit seines und des Wesens.*

because he has stepped before the countenance.

The fiery matter of all my capacity to will surging intractably,[8] everything possible for me revolving primevally,[9] intertwined and seemingly inseparable, the alluring glances of potentialities flaring up from every corner, the universe as a temptation, and I, born in an instant, both hands into the fire, deep into it, where the one that intends me is hidden, my deed, seized: now! And immediately the menace of the abyss is subdued; no longer a coreless multiplicity at play in the iridescent equality of its claims; but only two are left alongside each other, the other and the one, delusion and task.[1] But now the actualization commences within me. Having decided cannot mean that the one is done while the other remains lying there,[2] an extinguished mass, filling my soul, layer upon layer, with its dross. Only he that funnels all the force of the other into the doing of the one, absorbing into the actualization of what was chosen the undiminished passion of what was not chosen, only he that "serves God with the evil impulse," decides—and decides what happens. Once one has understood this, one also knows that precisely this deserves to be called righteous: that which is set right, toward which a man directs himself and for which he decides;[3] and if there were a devil he would not be the one who decided against God but he that in all eternity did not decide.

The man to whom freedom is guaranteed does not feel oppressed by causality. He knows that his mortal life is by its very nature an oscillation between You and It, and he senses the meaning of this. It suffices him that again and

[8] *unbändig.* Until 1957: *ungeheuer* (tremendously).
[9] *vorwelthaft kreisend.*
[1] *Auftrag.*
[2] *gelagert* (lying there) was inserted in 1957.
[3] *. . . das Gerechte zu nennen ist, das Gerichtete, wozu einer sich richtet und entscheidet.*

again he may set foot on the threshold of the sanctuary in
which he could never tarry. Indeed, having to leave it
again and again is for him an intimate part of the meaning
and destiny of this life. There, on the threshold, the response, the spirit is kindled in him again and again; here,
in the unholy and indigent land the spark has to prove
itself. What is here called necessity cannot frighten it; for
there he recognized true necessity: fate.

Fate and freedom are promised to each other. Fate is
encountered only by him that actualizes freedom. That I
discovered the deed that intends me, that, this movement
of my freedom, reveals the mystery to me. But this, too,
that I cannot accomplish it the way I intended it, this
resistance also reveals the mystery to me. He that forgets
all being caused as he decides from the depths, he that puts
aside possessions and cloak and steps bare before the countenance—this free human being encounters fate as the
counter-image of his freedom. It is not his limit but his
completion; freedom and fate embrace each other to form
meaning; and given meaning, fate—with its eyes, hitherto
severe, suddenly full of light—looks like grace itself.

No, the man who returns into the It-world, carrying the
spark, does not feel oppressed by causal necessity. And in
healthy ages, confidence flows to all the people from the
men of the spirit; to all of them, even the most obtuse, the
encounter, the presence has happened somehow, if only in
the dimension of nature, impulse, and twilight; all of them
have somewhere felt the You; and now the spirit interprets
this guarantee to them.

But in sick ages it happens that the It-world, no longer
irrigated and fertilized by the living currents of the You-
world, severed and stagnant, becomes a gigantic swamp
phantom and overpowers man. As he accommodates himself to a world of objects that no longer achieve any presence for him, he succumbs to it. Then common causality

grows into an oppressive and crushing doom.[4]

Every great culture that embraces more than one people rests upon some original encounter, an event at the source when a response was made to a You, an essential act of the spirit. Reinforced by the energy of subsequent generations that points in the same direction, this creates a distinctive conception of the cosmos in the spirit; only thus does a human cosmos[5] become possible again and again; only now can man again and again build houses of worship and human houses in a distinctive conception of space and from a confident soul—and fill vibrant time with new hymns and songs and give the human community itself a form. But only as long as he possesses this essential act in his own life, acting and suffering, only as long as he himself enters into the relation is he free and thus creative. When a culture is no longer centered in a living and continually renewed relational process, it freezes into the It-world which is broken only intermittently by the eruptive, glowing deeds of solitary spirits. From that point on, common causality, which hitherto was never able to disturb the spiritual conception of the cosmos, grows into an oppressive and crushing doom. Wise, masterful fate which, as long as it was attuned to the abundance of meaning in the cosmos, held sway over all causality, has become transformed into demonic absurdity[6] and has collapsed into causality. The same karma that appeared to earlier generations[7] as a beneficial dispensation—for our deeds[8] in this life raise us into higher spheres in the next—now is seen

---

[4] *Verhängnis.* "Doom" is used here only to render this word.
[5] *Kosmos des Menschen.* Before 1957: *Kosmos, gefasste Welt, heimische, haushafte Welt. Weltbehausung des Menschen:* cosmos, conceived world, homelike, houselike world, the world as man's dwellingplace . . .
[6] *zur sinnwidrigen Dämonie.*
[7] Buber's gloss, March 1937: in pre-Buddhistic India as opposed to Buddhistic India.
[8] Since 1957: our successes. This change weakens the contrast.

as tyranny; for the deeds of a former life of which we are
unconscious have imprisoned us in a dungeon from which
we cannot escape in this life. Where the meaningful law
of a heaven used to arch, with the spindle of necessity
hanging from its bright vault, the meaningless, tyrannical
power of the planets now holds sway. It used to be merely
a matter of entering *Dike*, the heavenly "path" that aimed
to be ours, too, and one could live with a free heart in the
total measure of destiny. Now we feel, whatever we do,
the compulsion of *heimarmene*,[9] a stranger to spirit who
bends every neck with the entire burden of the dead mass
of the world. The craving for redemption grows by leaps
and bounds and remains unsatisfied in the end, in spite of
all kinds of experiments, until it is finally assuaged by one
who teaches men how to escape from the wheel of rebirth,
or by one who saves the souls enslaved by the powers into
the freedom of the children of God. Such accomplish-
ments issue from a new encounter that becomes substantial, a new response of one human being to his You, an
event that comes to determine fate. The repercussions of
such a central essential act may include the supersession of
one culture by another that is devoted to this ray, but it is
also possible for a culture to be thus renewed.

The sickness of our age is unlike that of any other and
yet belongs with the sicknesses of all. The history of cultures is not a stadium of eons in which one runner after
another must cover the same circle of death, cheerfully and
unconsciously. A nameless path leads through their ascen-
sions and declines. It is not a path of progress and development. It is a descent through the spirals of the spiritual
underworld but could also be called an ascent to the inner-
most, subtlest, most intricate turn that knows no Beyond
and even less any Backward but only the unheard of re-

[9]A Greek word for fate, used by Plato, *Phaedo* 115a and *Gorgias* 512e.

turn[1]—the breakthrough. Shall we have to follow this path all the way to the end, to the test of the final darkness? But where there is danger what saves grows, too.[2]

The biologistic and the historiosophical orientations of this age, which made so much of their differences, have combined to produce a faith in doom that is more obdurate and anxious than any such faith has ever been. It is no longer the power of karma nor the power of the stars that rules man's lot ineluctably; many different forces claim this dominion, but upon closer examination it appears that most of our contemporaries believe in a medley of forces, as the late Romans believed in a medley of gods. The nature of these claims facilitates such a faith. Whether it is the "law of life"—a universal struggle in which everybody must either join the fight or renounce life—or the "psychological law" according to which innate drives[3] constitute the entire human soul; or the "social law" of an inevitable social process that is merely accompanied by will and consciousness; or the "cultural law" of an unalterably uniform genesis and decline of historical forms; or whatever variations there may be: the point is always that man is yoked into an inescapable process that he cannot resist, though he may be deluded enough to try. From the compulsion of the stars the ancient mysteries offered liberation; from the compulsion of karma, the Brahmanic sacrifice, accompanied by insight. Both were preparations for salvation. But the medley idol does not tolerate any faith in liberation. It is considered foolish to imagine any freedom; one is supposed to have nothing but the choice between reso-

[1]See pp. 35ff.
[2]A Quotation from Hölderlin's poem "Patmos," which begins: *Nah ist / Und schwer zu fassen der Gott./ Wo aber Gefahr ist, wächst / Das Rettende auch.* "Near is and hard to grasp the god. But where there is danger what saves grows, too."
[3]*eingebornen Gebrauchstrieben.*

lute and hopelessly rebellious slavery. Although all these
laws are frequently associated with long discussions of
teleological development and organic evolution, all of
them are based on the obsession with some running
down,[4] which involves unlimited causality. The dogma of
a gradual running down represents man's abdication in the
face of the proliferating It-world. Here the name of fate is
misused: fate is no bell that has been jammed down over
man; nobody encounters it, except those who started out
from freedom. But the dogma of some running down
leaves no room for freedom or for its most real revelation
whose tranquil strength changes the countenance of the
earth: returning. The dogma does not know the human
being who overcomes the universal struggle by returning;
who tears the web of drives, by returning; who rises above
the spell of his class by returning; who by returning stirs
up, rejuvenates, and changes the secure historical forms.
The dogma of running down offers you only one choice
as you face its game: to observe the rules or drop out. But
he that returns knocks over the men on the board. The
dogma will at most permit you to carry out conditionality

[4] *Ablauf: laufen* means running, and the prefix *ab*, like the Latin *de*,
means down. *Ablauf* can mean running off, drainage, as well as lapse (of
time) or expiration. When Schiller's Tell says, *Fort musst du, deine Uhr
ist abgelaufen*—words often quoted—he means: You have to go, your
clock's run down—or, a little less literally: You have to die, your time
is up. That *Ablauf* often suggests expiration, termination, and running
down is undeniable; whether Buber meant to emphasize these associations and whether he was thinking of entropy and the gradual running
down of the mechanistic universe is less clear. "Process"—the term
used in the first translation of the book—is misleading because such
so-called process philosophies as Bergson's and Whitehead's are not
mechanistic but stress freedom and creativity. (A few lines above,
where we have "an inevitable social process," Buber uses the German
Prozess.) Buber clearly associates *Ablauf* with "unlimited causality,"
with the "proliferating It-world," with the denial of freedom, *and with
doom*.

with your life and to "remain free" in your soul. But he that returns considers this freedom the most ignominious slavery.

Nothing can doom man but the belief in doom, for this prevents the movement of return.

The belief in doom is a delusion from the start. The scheme of running down is appropriate only for ordering that which is nothing-but-having-become, the severed world-event, objecthood[5] as history. The presence of the You, that which is born of association, is not accessible to this approach, which does not know the actuality of spirit; and this scheme is not valid for spirit. Divination based on objecthood is valid only for those who do not know presentness.[6] Whoever is overpowered by the It-world must consider the dogma of an ineluctable running down as a truth that creates a clearing in the jungle. In truth, this dogma only leads him deeper into the slavery of the It-world. But the world of the You is not locked up. Whoever proceeds toward it, concentrating his whole being, with his power to relate resurrected, beholds his freedom. And to gain freedom from the belief in unfreedom is to gain freedom.

*

One gains power over an incubus by addressing it by its real name. Similarly, the It-world that but now seemed to dwarf man's small strength with its uncanny power has to yield to anyone who recognizes its true nature: the particularization and alienation[7] of that out of whose abundance, welling up close by, every earthly You emerges to con-

[5] *Gegenständlichkeit.*
[6] *Gegenwärtigkeit.*
[7] *Versonderung und Verfremdung.*

front us—that which appeared to us at times as great and
terrible as the mother goddess, but nevertheless always
motherly.

—But how can we muster the strength to address the
incubus by his right name as long as a ghost lurks inside
us—the I that has been robbed of its actuality? How can
the buried power to relate be resurrected in a being in
which a vigorous ghost appears hourly to stamp down the
debris under which this power lies? How is a being to
collect itself as long as the mania of his detached I-hood[8]
chases it ceaselessly around an empty circle? How is anyone to behold his freedom if caprice[9] is his dwellingplace?

—Even as freedom and fate belong together, caprice
belongs with doom. But freedom and fate are promised to
each other and embrace each other to constitute meaning;
caprice and doom, the spook of the soul and the nightmare
of the world, get along with each other, living next door
and avoiding each other, without connection and friction,
at home in meaninglessness—until in one instant eye
meets eye, madly, and the confession erupts from both that
they are unredeemed. How much intellectual eloquence
and artistry is used today to prevent or at least conceal this
occurrence!

Free is the man that wills without caprice. He believes
in the actual, which is to say: he believes in the real[1] association of the real duality, I and You. He believes in destiny[2]
and also that it needs him. It does not lead him, it waits for
him. He must proceed toward it without knowing where
it waits for him. He must go forth with his whole being:
that he knows. It will not turn out the way his resolve

[8] *Ichheit.*
[9] *Willkür.*
[1] *reale.*
[2] *die Bestimmung.*

intended it; but what wants to come will come only if he resolves to do that which he can will. He must sacrifice his little will, which is unfree and ruled by things and drives, to his great will that moves away from being determined to find destiny.[3] Now he no longer interferes, nor does he merely allow things to happen. He listens to that which grows, to the way of Being in the world,[4] not in order to be carried along by it but rather in order to actualize it in the manner in which it, needing him, wants to be actualized by him—with human spirit and human deed, with human life and human death. He believes, I said; but this implies: he encounters.

The capricious man does not believe and encounter. He does not know association; he only knows the feverish world out there and his feverish desire to use it. We only have to give use an ancient, classical name, and it walks among the gods. When he says You, he means: You, my ability to use! And what he calls his destiny is merely an embellishment of and a sanction for his ability to use. In truth he has no destiny but is merely determined by things and drives, feels autocratic, and is capricious. He has no great will and tries to pass off caprice in its place. For sacrifice he lacks all capacity, however much he may talk of it, and you may recognize it by noting that he never becomes concrete. He constantly interferes, in order "to let it happen." How, he says to you, could one fail to assist destiny? How could one not employ all feasible means required for such an end? That is also how he sees those who are free; he cannot see them differently. But the free man does not have an end here and then fetch the means from there; he has only one thing: always only his resolve

---

[3] *vom Bestimmtsein weg und auf die Bestimmung zu.*
[4] *Er lauscht dem aus sich Werdenden, dem Weg des Wesens in der Welt.* In German, the fourfold alliteration recalls Richard Wagner.

to proceed toward his destiny. Having made this resolve, he will renew it at every fork in the road; and he would sooner believe that he was not really alive than he would believe that the resolve of the great will was insufficient and required the support of means. He believes; he encounters. But the unbelieving marrow of the capricious man cannot perceive anything but unbelief and caprice, positing ends and devising means. His world is devoid of sacrifice and grace, encounter and present, but shot through with ends and means: it could not be different and its name is doom. For all his autocratic bearing, he is inextricably entangled in unreality; and he becomes aware of this whenever he recollects his own condition. Therefore he takes pains to use the best part of his mind to prevent or at least obscure such recollection.[5]

But if this recollection of one's falling off,[6] of the deactualized and the actual I, were permitted to reach down to the roots that man calls despair and from which self-destruction and rebirth grow, this would be the beginning of the return.

*

The Brahmana of the hundred paths relates that the gods and the demons were once engaged in a contest. Then the demons said: "To whom shall we offer our sacrifices?" They placed all offerings in their own mouths. But the

[5] *Besinnung* can also mean consciousness or reflection; *sich besinnen* can mean to recollect or remember; and *zur Besinnung kommen*, to recover one's senses. Overtones of this last meaning are present here. This passage and the next paragraph invite comparison with Kierkegaard's *Sickness Unto Death* and—like much of *Ich und Du*—with Heidegger's *Being and Time.*

[6] *das Abgefallensein:* literally, the state of having fallen off or away; *abfallen* can also suggest defection and apostasy. Cf. "O Hamlet, what a falling-off was there" (*Hamlet*, Act I, scene 5, line 47).

gods placed the offerings in one another's mouth. Then Prajapati, the primal spirit, bestowed himself upon the gods.

*

—One can understand how the It-world, left to itself, untouched and unthawed by the emergence of any You, should become alienated and turn into an incubus; but how does it happen that, as you say, the I of man is deactualized? Whether it lives in relation or outside it, the I remains assured of itself in its self-consciousness, which is a strong thread of gold on which the changing states are strung. Whether I say, "I see you" or "I see the tree," seeing may not be equally actual in both cases, but the I is equally actual in both.

—Let us examine, let us examine ourselves to see whether this is so. The linguistic form proves nothing. After all, many a spoken You really means an It to which one merely says You from habit, thoughtlessly. And many a spoken It really means a You whose presence one may remember with one's whole being, although one is far away. Similarly, there are innumerable occasions when I is only an indispensable pronoun, only a necessary abbreviation for "This one there who is speaking." But self-consciousness? If one sentence truly intends the You of a relation and the other one the It of an experience, and if the I in both sentences is thus intended in truth, do both sentences issue from the same self-consciousness?

The I of the basic word I-You is different from that of the basic word I-It.

The I of the basic word I-It appears as an ego[7] and

[7] *Eigenwesen*, literally own-being or self-being, is a highly unusual word. In the first English version of the book it has been rendered as "individuality" although Buber had expressly protested on seeing page proofs that this bothered him a great deal (*"stört mich doch sehr"*): "But I cannot

becomes conscious of itself as a subject (of experience and use).

The I of the basic word I-You appears as a person and becomes conscious of itself as subjectivity (without any dependent genetive).[8]

Egos appear by setting themselves apart from other egos.

Persons appear by entering into relation to other persons.

One is the spiritual form of natural differentiation, the other that of natural association.

The purpose of setting oneself apart is to experience and use, and the purpose of that is "living"—which means dying one human life long.

The purpose of relation is the relation itself—touching

---

think of anything better. In French there is the word *égotiste* (cf. Stendhal) which comes close to what I mean; but the English *egotist* unfortunately means *Egoist*, and that is something else. Would it perhaps be possible to say: the egotical being??" Except for the last three words, the comment was written in German, and in a covering letter, dated March 8, 1937, Buber devoted another whole paragraph to this problem.

He insisted that he had nothing against individualities and added: "*Eigenwesen*, on the other hand, refers to a man's relation to himself. I do hope that you will find it possible after all to translate it differently, perhaps by moving in the direction suggested in the enclosure."

"Ego" works perfectly in all the many passages in which Buber speaks of *Eigenwesen*, including the paragraph after the next one in which "egotist," for example, would not do at all. The only serious objection that comes to mind is that those who read Freud or subsequent psychoanalytic literature in English may have irrelevant and distracting associations with the word "ego." But this objection loses all force when we recall that the term Freud himself used was *Ich* (cf. *Das Ich und das Es*)—the very same word that Buber uses constantly in *Ich und Du* in an altogether difference sense. Buber's *Ich* is closer to ordinary usage than Freud's; and "ego" in the following pages is closer to ordinary English usage than is the Freudian "ego."

[8] I.e., without any "of" clause like that in the preceding parenthesis; also without any object.

the You. For as soon as we touch a You, we are touched
by a breath of eternal life.[9]

Whoever stands in relation, participates in an actuality;
that is, in a being that is neither merely a part of him nor
merely outside him. All actuality is an activity in which I
participate without being able to appropriate it. Where
there is no participation, there is no actuality. Where there
is self-appropriation, there is no actuality. The more directly the You is touched, the more perfect is the participation.

The I is actual through its participation in actuality. The
more perfect the participation is, the more actual the I
becomes.

But the I that steps out of the event of the relation into
detachment and the self-consciousness accompanying
that, does not lose its actuality. Participation remains in it
as a living potentiality. To use words that originally refer
to the highest relation but may also be applied to all others:
the seed remains in him. This is the realm of subjectivity
in which the I apprehends simultaneously its association
and its detachment. Genuine subjectivity can be understood only dynamically, as the vibration of the I in its
lonely truth. This is also the place where the desire for
ever higher and more unconditional relation and for
perfect participation in being arises and keeps rising. In
subjectivity the spiritual substance of the person ma-
tures.

The person becomes conscious of himself as participat-
ing in being, as being-with, and thus as a being. The ego
becomes conscious of himself as being this way and not
that. The person says, "I am"; the ego says, "That is how
I am." "Know thyself" means to the person: know yourself as being. To the ego it means: know your being-that-

[9]Until 1957: of the You, that is, of eternal life.

way. By setting himself apart from others, the ego moves away from being.

This does not mean that the person "gives up" his being-that-way, his being different; only, this is not the decisive perspective but merely the necessary and meaningful form of being. The ego, on the other hand, wallows in his being-that-way—or rather for the most part in the fiction of his being-that-way—a fiction that he has devised for himself. For at bottom self-knowledge usually means to him the fabrication of an effective apparition of the self that has the power to deceive him ever more thoroughly; and through the contemplation and veneration of this apparition one seeks the semblance of knowledge of one's own being-that-way, while actual knowledge of it would lead one to self-destruction—or rebirth.

The person beholds his self; the ego occupies himself with his My: my manner, my race, my works, my genius.

The ego does not participate in any actuality nor does he gain any. He sets himself apart from everything else and tries to possess as much as possible by means of experience and use. That is *his* dynamics: setting himself apart and taking possession—and the object is always It, that which is not actual. He knows himself as a subject, but this subject can appropriate as much as it wants to, it will never gain any substance: it remains like a point, functional, that which experiences, that which uses, nothing more. All of its extensive and multifarious being-that-way, all of its eager "individuality" cannot help it to gain any substance.

There are not two kinds of human beings, but there are two poles of humanity.

No human being is pure person, and none is pure ego; none is entirely actual, none entirely lacking in actuality. Each lives in a twofold I. But some men are so person-oriented that one may call them persons, while others are so ego-oriented that one may call them egos. Between these and those true history takes place.

The more a human being, the more humanity is dominated by the ego, the more does the I fall prey to inactuality. In such ages the person in the human being and in humanity comes to lead a subterranean, hidden, as it were invalid existence—until it is summoned.

*

How much of a person a man is depends on how strong the I of the basic word I-You is in the human duality of his I.

The way he says I—what he means when he says I—decides where a man belongs and where he goes. The word "I" is the true shibboleth of humanity.

Listen to it!

How dissonant the I of the ego[1] sounds! When it issues from tragic lips, tense with some self-contradiction that they try to hold back, it can move us to great pity. When it issues from chaotic lips that savagely, heedlessly, unconsciously represent contradiction, it can make us shudder. When the lips are vain and smooth, it sounds embarrassing or disgusting.

Those who pronounce the severed I, wallowing in the capital letter, uncover the shame of the world spirit that has been debased to mere spirituality.

But how beautiful and legitimate the vivid and emphatic I of Socrates sounds! It is the I of infinite conversation, and the air of conversation is present on all its ways, even before his judges, even in the final hour in prison. This I lived in that relation to man which is embodied in conversation. It believed in the actuality of men and went out

[1] *des Eigenmenschen.*

toward them. Thus it stood together with them in actuality
and is never severed from it. Even solitude cannot spell
forsakenness, and when the human world falls silent for
him, he hears his *daimonion* say You.

How beautiful and legitimate the full I of Goethe
sounds! It is the I of pure intercourse with nature. Nature
yields to it and speaks ceaselessly with it; she reveals her
mysteries to it and yet does not betray her mystery. It
believes in her and says to the rose: "So it is You"—and
at once shares the same actuality with the rose. Hence,
when it returns to itself, the spirit of actuality stays with
it; the vision of the sun clings to the blessed eye that recalls
its own likeness to the sun, and the friendship of the elements accompanies man into the calm of dying and
rebirth.[2]

Thus the "adequate, true, and pure" I-saying of the rep-
resentatives of association, the Socratic and the Goethean
persons, resounds through the ages.

And to anticipate and choose an image from the realm
of unconditional relation: how powerful, even overpower-
ing, is Jesus' I-saying, and how legitimate to the point of
being a matter of course! For it is the I of the unconditional
relation in which man calls his You "Father" in such a way
that he himself becomes nothing but a son. Whenever he
says I, he can only mean the I of the holy basic word that
has become unconditional for him. If detachment ever
touches him, it is surpassed by association, and it is from
this that he speaks to others. In vain you seek to reduce this

[2]Buber alludes to three Goethe poems: "Blessed eye" echoes *Faust*, line
11300, the song of Lynceus. Then, one of Goethe's late *Xenien* (1823:
Book III): "Were not the eye so like the sun, / It never could behold
the sun: / If the god's own power did not lie in us, / How could that
which is godlike delight us?" And the final stanza of "Blessed Yearning"
in Goethe's *Divan:* "And until you have possessed / dying and rebirth,
/ you are but a sullen guest / on the gloomy earth."

I to something that derives its power from itself, nor can you limit this You to anything that dwells in us. Both would once again deactualize the actual, the present relation. I and You remain; everyone can speak the You and then becomes I; everyone can say Father and then becomes son; actuality abides.

*

—But what if a man's mission requires him to know only his association with his cause and no real relation to any You, no present encounter with any You, so that everything around him becomes It and subservient to his cause? How about the I-saying of Napoleon? Wasn't that legitimate? Is this phenomenon of experiencing and using no person?

—Indeed, this master of the[3] age evidently did not know the dimension of the You. The matter has been put well: all being was for him *valore.*[4] Gently, he compared the followers who denied him after his fall with Peter; but there was nobody whom *he* could have denied, for there was nobody whom he recognized as a being. He was the demonic You for the millions and did not respond; to "You" he responded by saying: It; he responded fictitiously on the personal level—responding only in his own sphere, that of his cause, and only with his deeds. This is the elementary historical barrier at which the basic word of association loses its reality, the character of reciprocity: the demonic You for whom nobody can become a You. This third type, in addition to the person and the ego, to the free and the arbitrary man—not between them—oc-

[3]Buber in March 1937 protested against "his age," insisted on *"the* age," and added that it was our age, too.
[4]Value. But the Italian word can also mean worth, courage, fitness.

curs in fateful eminence in fateful times: ardently, everything flames toward him while he himself stands in a cold
fire; a thousand relations reach out toward him but none
issues from him. He participates in no actuality, but others
participate immeasurably in him as in an actuality.

To be sure, he views the beings around him as so many
machines capable of different achievements that have to be
calculated and used for the cause. But that is also how he
views himself (only he can never cease experimenting to
determine his own capacities, and yet never experiences
their limits). He treats himself, too, as an It.

Thus his I-saying is not vitally emphatic, not full. Much
less does it feign these qualities (like the I-saying of the
modern ego).[5] He does not even speak of himself, he
merely speaks "on his own behalf." The I spoken and
written by him is the required subject of the sentences that
convey his statements and orders—no more and no less. It
lacks subjectivity; neither does it have a self-consciousness
that is preoccupied with being-that-way; and least of all
does it have any delusions about its own appearance. "I am
the clock that exists and does not know itself ": thus he
himself formulated his fatefulness, the actuality of this phenomenon and the inactuality of this I, after he had been
separated from his cause;[6] for it was only then that he
could, and had to, think and speak of himself and recollect
his I which appeared only then. What appears is not mere
subject; neither does it reach subjectivity: the magic spell
broken, but unredeemed, it finds expression in the terrible
word, as legitimate as it is illegitimate: "The universe con-
templates Us!" In the end it sinks back into mystery.

Who, after such a step and such a fall,[7] would dare to

[5] *Eigenmenschen.*
[6] *aus seiner Sache.*
[7] *Untergang.*

claim that this man understood his tremendous, mon-
strous[8] mission—or that he misunderstood it? What is certain is that the age for which the demonic man who lives
without a present has become master and model will
misunderstand him. It fails to see that what holds sway
here is destiny and accomplishment, not the lust for and
delight in power.[9] It goes into ecstasies over the command-
ing brow and has no inkling of the signs inscribed upon
this forehead like digits upon the face of a clock. One tries
studiously to imitate the way he looked at others, without
any understanding of his need and necessitation, and one
mistakes the objective severity of this I for fermenting
self-awareness. The word "I" remains the shibboleth of
humanity. Napoleon spoke it without the power to relate,
but he did speak it as the I of an accomplishment.[1] Those
who exert themselves to copy this, merely betray the hopelessness of their own self-contradiction.

*

—What is that: self-contradiction?
—When man does not test the *a priori* of relation in the
world, working out and actualizing the innate You in what
he encounters, it turns inside. Then it unfolds through the
unnatural, impossible object, the I—which is to say that it
unfolds where there is no room for it to unfold. Thus the
confrontation within the self comes into being, and this
cannot be relation, presence, the current of reciprocity,
but only self-contradiction. Some men may try to interpret
this as a relation, perhaps one that is religious, in order to
extricate themselves from the horror of their *Doppelgänger:*

[8] *ungeheure, ungeheuerliche.*
[9] *Schickung und Vollzug, nicht Machtbrunst und Machtgenuss.*
[1] *als das Ich eines Vollzugs.*

they are bound to keep rediscovering the deception of any such interpretation. Here is the edge of life. What is unfulfilled has here escaped into the mad delusion of some fulfillment; now it gropes around in the labyrinth and gets lost ever more profoundly.

*

At times when man is overcome by the horror of the alienation between I and world, it occurs to him that something might be done. Imagine that at some dreadful midnight you lie there, tormented by a waking dream:[2] the bulwarks have crumbled and the abysses scream, and you realize in the midst of this agony that life is still there and I must merely get through to it—but how? how? Thus feels man in the hours when he collects himself:[3] overcome by horror, pondering, without direction. And yet he may know the right direction, deep down in the unloved knowledge of the depths—the direction of return that leads through sacrifice. But he rejects this knowledge; what is "mystical" cannot endure the artificial midnight sun.[4] He summons thought in which he places, quite rightly, much confidence: thought is supposed to fix everything. After all, it is the lofty art of thought that it can paint a reliable and practically credible picture of the world. Thus man says to his thought: "Look at the dreadful shape that lies over there with those cruel eyes—is she not the

[2]Buber in March 1937: "one really dreams; i.e., one is under the spell of a dream although one is awake."
[3]*in den Stunden der Besinnung.*
[4]*der elektrischen Sonne.* Buber's gloss, March 1937, in German except for the last six words: "regarding the 'electric sun': it is midnight; the man told about here had lit the strong electric light on the ceiling, this small sun, as a defense against the torment of the waking dream; but it is at the same time a symbol for the 'thought' he invokes. Hence perhaps: cannot resist the sunlike electric lamp."

one with whom I played long ago? Do you remember how she used to laugh at me with these eyes and how good they were then? And now look at my wretched I—I'll admit it to you: it is empty, and whatever I put into myself, experience as well as use, does not penetrate to this cavern. Won't you fix things between her and me so that she relents and I get well again?" And thought, ever obliging and skillful, paints with its accustomed speed a series— nay, two series of pictures on the right and the left wall. Here is (or rather: happens, for the world pictures of thought are reliable motion pictures) the universe. From the whirl of the stars emerges the small earth, from the teeming on earth emerges small man, and now history carries him forth through the ages, to persevere in rebuilding the anthills of the cultures that crumble under its steps. Beneath this series of pictures is written: "One and all." On the other wall happens the soul. A female figure spins the orbits of all stars and the life of all creatures and the whole of world history; all is spun with a single thread and is no longer called stars and creatures and world but feelings and representations or even living experiences and states of the soul. And beneath this series of pictures is written: "One and all."

Henceforth, when man is for once overcome by the horror of alienation and the world fills him with anxiety, he looks up (right or left, as the case may be) and sees a picture. Then he sees that the I is contained in the world, and that there really is no I, and thus the world cannot harm the I, and he calms down; or he sees that the world is contained in the I, and that there really is no world, and thus the world cannot harm the I, and he calms down. And when man is overcome again by the horror of alienation and the I fills him with anxiety, he looks up and sees a picture; and whichever he sees, it does not matter, either the empty I is stuffed full of world or it is submerged in the flood of the world, and he calms down.

But the moment will come, and it is near, when man, overcome by horror, looks up and in a flash sees both pictures at once. And he is seized by a deeper horror.

Third Part

EXTENDED, the lines of relationships intersect in the eternal You.

Every single You is a glimpse of that. Through every single You the basic word addresses the eternal You. The mediatorship of the You of all beings accounts for the fullness of our relationships to them—and for the lack of fulfillment. The innate You is actualized each time without ever being perfected. It attains perfection solely in the immediate relationship to the You that in accordance with its nature cannot become an It.

Men have addressed their eternal You by many names. When they sang of what they had thus named, they still meant You: the first myths were hymns of praise. Then the names entered into the It-language; men felt impelled more and more to think of and to talk about their eternal You as an It. But all names of God remain hallowed—because they have been used not only to speak *of* God but also to speak *to* him.

Some would deny any legitimate use of the word God because it has been misused so much. Certainly it is the most burdened of all human words. Precisely for that reason it is the most imperishable and unavoidable.[1] And how

[1] *das unvergänglichste und unumgänglichste.*

much weight has all erroneous talk about God's nature and works (although there never has been nor can be any such talk that is not erroneous) compared with the one truth that all men who have addressed God really meant him? For whoever pronounces the word God and really means You, addresses, no matter what his delusion, the true You of his life that cannot be restricted by any other and to whom he stands in a relationship that includes all others.

But whoever abhors the name and fancies[2] that he is godless—when he addresses with his whole devoted being the You of his life that cannot be restricted by any other, he addresses God.

*

When we walk our way and encounter a man who comes toward us, walking his way, we know our way only and not his; for his comes to life for us only in the encounter.

Of the perfect relational process we know in the manner of having lived through it our going forth, our way. The other part merely happens to us, we do not know it. It happens to us in the encounter. But we try to lift more than we can if we speak of it as something beyond the encounter.

Our concern, our care must be not for the other side but for our own, not for grace but for will. Grace concerns us insofar as we proceed toward it and await its presence; it is not our object.[3]

The You confronts me. But I enter into a direct relationship to it. Thus the relationship is at once being chosen and

[2] *wähnt.* Until 1957: *glaubt* (believes).
[3] The immediately following paragraph was omitted in 1957: "What we know of the way by virtue of our having lived, by virtue of our life, is not a waiting, not a being open."

choosing, passive and active. For an action of the whole being does away with all partial actions and thus also with all sensations of action (which depend entirely on the limited nature of actions)—and hence it comes to resemble passivity.

This is the activity of the human being who has become whole: it has been called not-doing, for nothing particular, nothing partial is at work in man and thus nothing of him intrudes into the world. It is the whole human being, closed in its wholeness, at rest in its wholeness, that is active here, as the human being has become an active whole. When one has achieved steadfastness in this state, one is able to venture forth toward the supreme encounter.

To this end one does not have to strip away the world of the senses as a world of appearance. There is no world of appearance, there is only the world—which, to be sure, appears twofold to us in accordance with our twofold attitude. Only the spell of separation needs to be broken. Nor is there any need to "go beyond sense experience"; any experience, no matter how spiritual, could only yield us an It. Nor need we turn to a world of ideas and values—that cannot become present for us. All this is not needed. Can one say what is needed? Not by way of a prescription. All the prescriptions that have been excogitated and invented in the ages of the human spirit, all the preparations, exercises, and meditations[4] that have been suggested have

---

[4] *Versenkung.* Buber in March 1937: "Instead of 'absorption' better 'meditation' at this point (what is meant is the Buddhistic *dhyaya*)." What he meant was *dhyana.* I had "meditations" before reading this and have naturally let it stand. But a little later on, when *Versenkung* is used repeatedly in a broader sense, I have rendered it consistently by "immersion," which is not only better than "absorption" but just right. In the first passage in which the term is introduced in this sense, it is equated with "a descent into the self."

Moreover, *immerse,* like *versenken,* can be transitive or reflexive, and in both languages the meaning intended is the reflexive one: I immerse

nothing to do with the primally simple fact of encounter. All the advantages for knowledge or power that one may owe to one or another exercise do not approach that of which we are speaking here. All this has its place in the It-world and does not take us one step—does not take the decisive step—out of it. Going forth is unteachable in the sense of prescriptions. It can only be indicated—by drawing a circle that excludes everything else. Then the one thing needful becomes visible: the total acceptance of the present.

To be sure, this acceptance involves a heavier risk and a more fundamental return, the further man has lost his way in separation. What has to be given up is not the I, as most mystics suppose: the I is indispensable for any relationship, including the highest, which always presupposes an I and You. What has to be given up is not the I but that false drive for self-affirmation[5] which impels man to flee from the unreliable, unsolid, unlasting, unpredictable, dangerous world of relation into the having of things.

*

Every actual relationship to another being[6] in the world is exclusive. Its You is freed and steps forth to confront us in its uniqueness. It fills the firmament—not as if there were nothing else, but everything else lives in *its* light. As

myself. When I am immersed or in a state of immersion, this is a result of my effort. And the ultimate outcome may be that I am drowned and my I is annulled; or as a Buddhist scripture has it, "he is gone to annihilation."

[5] *Selbstbehauptungstriebs:* the term is somewhat unusual, although *Selbsterhaltungstrieb* (the drive or instinct of self-preservation) is quite common. It is doubly remarkable that Heidegger entitled his inaugural lecture as Rector of the University of Freiburg, in which he embraced Nazism, *Die Selbstbehauptung der deutschen Universität* (1933).

[6] *zu einem Wesen oder einer Wesenheit:* in English the single word "being" must serve for both terms.

long as the presence of the relationship endures, this world-wideness cannot be infringed. But as soon as a You becomes an It, the world-wideness of the relationship appears as an injustice against the world, and its exclusiveness as an exclusion of the universe.

In the relation to God, unconditional exclusiveness and unconditional inclusiveness are one. For those who enter into the absolute relationship, nothing particular retains any importance—neither things nor beings, neither earth nor heaven—but everything is included in the relationship. For entering into the pure relationship does not involve ignoring everything but seeing everything in the You, not renouncing the world but placing it upon its proper ground. Looking away from the world is no help toward God; staring at the world is no help either; but whoever beholds the world in him stands in his presence. "World here, God there"—that is It-talk; and "God in the world"—that, too, is It-talk; but leaving out nothing, leaving nothing behind, to comprehend all—all the world—in comprehending the You, giving the world its due and truth, to have nothing besides God but to grasp everything in him, that is the perfect relationship.

One does not find God if one remains in the world; one does not find God if one leaves the world. Whoever goes forth to his You with his whole being and carries to it all the being of the world, finds him whom one cannot seek.

Of course, God is "the wholly other"; but he is also the wholly same: the wholly present. Of course, he is the *mysterium tremendum* that appears and overwhelms; but he is also the mystery of the obvious that is closer to me than my own I.[7]

When you fathom the life of things and of conditional-

---

[7]Rudolf Otto had argued in *Das Heilige* (1917; translated as *The Idea of the Holy*, 1923) that God is "the wholly other" and experienced as a *mysterium tremendum.*

ity, you reach the indissoluble; when you dispute the life of things and of conditionality, you wind up before the nothing; when you consecrate life you encounter the living God.

*

The You-sense of the man who in his relationships to all individual Yous experiences the disappointment of the change into It, aspires beyond all of them and yet not all the way toward his eternal You. Not the way one seeks something: in truth, there is no God-seeking because there is nothing where one could not find him. How foolish and hopeless must one be to leave one's way of life to seek God: even if one gained all the wisdom of solitude and all the power of concentration, one would miss him. It is rather as if a man went his way and merely wished that it might be *the* way; his aspiration finds expression in the strength of his wish. Every encounter is a way station that grants him a view of fulfillment; in each he thus fails to share, and yet also does share, in the one because he is ready. Ready, not seeking, he goes his way; this gives him the serenity toward all things and the touch that helps them. But once he has found, his heart does not turn away from them although he now encounters everything in the one. He blesses all the cells that have sheltered him as well as all those where he will still put up. For this finding is not an end of the way but only its eternal center.

It is a finding without seeking; a discovery of what is most original and the origin. The You-sense that cannot be satiated until it finds the infinite You sensed its presence from the beginning; this presence merely had to become wholly actual for it out of the actuality of the consecrated life of the world.

It is not as if God could be inferred from anything—say, from nature as its cause, or from history as its helmsman, or perhaps from the subject as the self that thinks itself through it. It is not as if something else were "given" and this were then deduced from it. This is what confronts us immediately and first and always, and legitimately it can only be addressed, not asserted.

*

The essential element in our relationship to God has been sought in a feeling that has been called a feeling of dependence[8] or, more recently, in an attempt to be more precise, creature-feeling.[9] While the insistence on this element and its definition are right, the onesided emphasis on this factor leads to a misunderstanding of the character of the perfect relationship.

What has been said earlier of love is even more clearly true at this point: feelings merely accompany the fact[1] of the relationship which after all is established not in the soul but between an I and a You. However essential one considers a feeling, it still remains subject to the dynamics of the soul where one feeling is surpassed, excelled, and replaced by another; feelings, unlike relationships, can be compared on a scale. Above all, every feeling has its place in a polar tension; it derives its color and meaning not from itself alone but also from its polar opposite; every feeling is conditioned by its opposite. Actually, the absolute relationship includes all relative relationships and is, unlike them, no longer a part but the whole in which all of them are consummated and become one. But in psychology the

[8] By F. E. D. Schleiermacher.
[9] By Rudolf Otto.
[1] Until 1957: the metaphysical and metapsychical fact.

absolute relationship is relativized by being derived from a particular and limited feeling that is emphasized.

If one starts out from the soul, the perfect relationship can only be seen as bipolar, as *coincidentia oppositorum*, as the fusion of opposite feelings. Of course, as one looks back one pole frequently disappears, suppressed by the basic religious orientation of the person, and it is only in the purest and most open-minded and profound introspection that it can be recalled.

Yes, in the pure relationship you felt altogether dependent, as you could never possibly feel in any other—and yet also altogether free as never and nowhere else; created—and creative. You no longer felt the one, limited by the other; you felt both without bounds, both at once.

That you need God more than anything, you know at all times in your heart. But don't you know also that God needs you—in the fullness of his eternity, you? How would man exist if God did not need him, and how would you exist? You need God in order to be, and God needs you—for that which is the meaning of your life. Teachings and poems try to say more, and say too much: how murky and presumptuous is the chatter of "the emerging God"—but the emergence of the living God we know unswervingly in our hearts.[2] The world is not divine play, it is divine fate. That there are world, man, the human person, you and I, has divine meaning.

Creation—happens to us, burns into us, changes us, we tremble and swoon, we submit. Creation—we participate in it, we encounter the creator,[3] offer ourselves to him, helpers and companions.

Two great servants move through the ages: prayer and sacrifice. In prayer man pours himself out, dependent

[2] *vom "werdenden Gott"—aber ein Werden des seienden Gottes ist, . . .*
[3] *dem Schaffenden:* this is not the theological term for the Creator.

without reservation, knowing that, incomprehensibly, he acts on God, albeit without exacting anything from God;[4] for when he no longer covets anything for himself, he beholds his effective activity burning in the supreme flame. And those who sacrifice? I cannot despise the honest servants of the remote past who thought that God desired the smell of their burnt sacrifices: they knew in a foolish and vigorous way that one can and should give to God; and that is also known to him who offers his little will to God and encounters him in a great will. "Let your will be done"— is all he says, but truth goes on to say for him: "through me whom you need." What distinguishes sacrifice and prayer from all magic? Magic wants to be effective without entering into any relationship and performs its arts in the void, while sacrifice and prayer step "before the countenance," into the perfection of the sacred basic word that signifies reciprocity. They say You and listen.

Wishing to understand the pure relationship as dependence means wishing to deactualize one partner of the relationship and thus the relationship itself.

*

The same thing happens if one starts from the opposite side and finds the essential element of the religious act in immersion[5] or a descent into the self—whether the self is to be stripped of all subjectivity and I-hood or whether the self is to be understood as the One that thinks and is. The former view supposes that God will enter the being that has been freed of I-hood or that at that point one merges into God; the other view supposes that one stands immedi-

[4] *auf Gott wirken, wenn auch nicht eben von Gott erwirken.* "Effective activity" later in the same sentence: *Wirken.*
[5] *Versenkung.* See note 4 on pp. 125f.

ately in oneself as the divine One. Thus the first holds that
in a supreme moment all You-saying ends because there is
no longer any duality; the second, that there is no truth in
You-saying at all because in truth there is no duality. The
first believes in the unification,[6] the second in the identity
of the human and the divine. Both insist on what is beyond
I and You: for the first this comes to be, perhaps in ecstasy,
while for the second it is there all along and reveals itself,
perhaps as the thinking subject beholds its self. Both annul
relationship—the first, as it were, dynamically, as the I is
swallowed by the You, which now ceases to be a You and
becomes the only being; the second, as it were, statically,
as the I is freed, becomes a self, and recognizes itself as the
only being. The doctrine of dependence considers the I-
supporter of the world-arch of pure relation as so weak and
insignificant that his ability to support the arch ceases to
be credible, while the one doctrine of immersion does
away altogether with the arch in its perfection and the
other one treats it as a chimera that has to be overcome.

The doctrines of immersion invoke the great epigrams
of identification—one of them above all the Johannine "I
and the Father are one,"[7] and the other one the doctrine
of Sandilya: "The All-embracing is my self in the inner
heart."[8]

The paths of these two epigrams are diametrically opposed. The former (after a long subterranean course) has
its source in the myth-sized life of a person and then unfolds in a doctrine. The second emerges in a doctrine and

[6] *Vereinigung.*
[7] John 10:30.
[8] Khandogya Upanishad, III. 14. 4: "He from whom all works, all
desires, all sweet odours and tastes proceed, who embraces all this, who
never speaks and who is never surprised, he, my self within the heart,
is that Brahma(n). . . . thus said Sandilya, yea, thus he said" (transl. Max
Müller).

culminates (provisionally) in the myth-sized life of a person. On these paths the character of each epigram is changed. The Christ of the Johannine tradition, the Word that has become flesh but once, takes us to Eckhart's Christ whom God begets eternally in the human soul. The formula of the coronation of the self in the Upanishads—"That is the actual, it is the self, and that you are"[9] takes us far more quickly to the Buddhistic formula of deposition: "A self and what pertains to the self are not to be found in truth and actuality."

Beginning and end of both paths have to be considered separately.

That there is no justification for invoking the "are one"[1] is obvious for anyone who reads the Gospel according to John without skipping and with an open mind. It is really nothing less than the Gospel of the pure relationship. There are truer things here than the familiar mystic verse: "I am you, and you are I." The father and the son, being consubstantial—we may say: God and man, being consubstantial, are actually and forever Two, the two partners of the primal relationship that, from God to man, is called mission and commandment; from man to God, seeing and hearing; between both, knowledge and love. And in this relationship the son, although the father dwells and works in him, bows before him that is "greater" and prays to him. All modern attempts to reinterpret this primal actuality of dialogue and to make of it a relationship of the I to the self or something of that sort, as if it were a process confined to man's self-sufficient inwardness, are vain and belong to the abysmal history of deactualization.

[9]Khandogya Upanishad VI. 8.7: "It is the True. It is the Self, and thou, O Svetaketu, art it" (transl. Max Müller). This refrain is repeated in VI. 9.4, 10.3, 11.3, 12.3, 13.3, 14.3, 15.2, and 16.3.
[1]Before 1957 the two words were printed in Greek: *hen esmen.*

—But mysticism? It relates how unity within duality feels. Have we any right to doubt the faithfulness of this testimony?

—I know not only of one but of two kinds of events in which one is no longer aware of any duality. Mysticism sometimes confounds them, as I, too, did at one time.

First, the soul may become one. This event occurs not between man and God but in man. All forces are concentrated into the core, everything that would distract them is pulled in, and the being stands alone in itself and jubilates, as Paracelsus put it, in its exaltation. This is a man's decisive moment. Without this he is not fit for the work of the spirit. With this—it is decided deep down whether this means preparation or sufficient satisfaction. Concentrated into a unity, a human being can proceed to his encounter —wholly successful only now—with mystery and perfection. But he can also savor the bliss of his unity and, without incurring the supreme duty, return into distraction. Everything along our way is decision—intentional, dimly sensed, or altogether secret—but this one, deep down, is the primally secret decision, pregnant with the most powerful destiny.

The other event is that unfathomable kind of relational act itself in which one has the feeling that Two have become One: "one and one made one, bare shineth in bare."[2] I and You drown; humanity that but now confronted the deity is absorbed into it; glorification, deification, universal unity have appeared. But when one returns into the wretchedness of daily turmoil, transfigured and exhausted, and with a knowing heart reflects on both, is one not bound to feel that Being is split, with one part abandoned to hopelessness? What help is it to my soul that it can be

---

[2] *"ein und ein vereinet da liubtet bloz in bloz"* (Master Eckhart).

transported again from this world into that unity,[3] when this world itself has, of necessity, no share whatever in that unity—what does all "enjoyment of God" profit a life rent in two? If that extravagantly rich heavenly Moment has nothing to do with my poor earthly moment—what is it to me as long as I still have to live on earth—must in all seriousness still live on earth? That is the way to understand those masters who renounced the raptures of the ecstasy of "unification."[4]

Which was no unification. Those human beings may serve as a metaphor who in the passion of erotic fulfillment are so carried away by the miracle of the embrace that all knowledge of I and You drowns in the feeling of a unity that neither exists nor can exist. What the ecstatic calls unification is the rapturous dynamics of the relationship; not a unity that has come into being at this moment in world time, fusing I and You, but the dynamics of the relationship itself which can stand before the two carriers of this relationship, although they confront each other immovably, and cover the eyes of the enraptured.[5] What we find here is a marginal[6] exorbitance of the act of relation: the relationship itself in its vital unity is felt so vehemently that its members pale in the process: its life predominates so much that the I and the You between whom it is established are forgotten. This is one of the phenomena that we find on the margins where actuality becomes blurred. But what is greater for us than all enigmatic webs at the margins of being is the central actuality of an everyday hour on earth, with a streak of sunshine on a maple

[3] *Einheit.*
[4] *"Einungs"-Ekstase.*
[5] Buber in March 1937, in English: "and cover each of them to the feeling of the enraptured other one" (*sic*).
[6] *Ibid.*, Buber protested against "fringe" and suggested that here and in a few other passages *Rand* might be translated "brink."

twig and an intimation of the eternal You.

Against this stands the claim of the other doctrine of immersion that at heart the universe and the self are identical and hence no You-saying can ever grant any ultimate actuality.

This claim is answered by the doctrine itself. One of the Upanishads relates how Indra, the prince of the gods, comes to Prajapati, the creator spirit, to learn how one can find and recognize the self. He remains a student for a century and is twice sent away with inadequate information, before he finally attains the right information: "When one rests in a deep sleep, without dreams, that is the self, the immortal, the assured, the All-being." Indra goes hence but is soon troubled by a scruple. He returns and asks: "In that state, O sublime one, we do not know of our self, 'That am I'; neither, 'Those are the beings.' We are gone to annihilation. I see no profit here." "That, my lord, is indeed how it is," replies Prajapati.[7]

Insofar as this doctrine contains an assertion about true being, we cannot find out in this life whether the doctrine is true; but however that may be, there is one thing with which this doctrine has nothing in common: lived actuality; and it therefore has to demote this to the level of a merely illusory world. And insofar as this doctrine contains directions for immersion in true being, it does not lead into lived actuality but into "annihilation," in which there is no consciousness, from which no memory survives—and· the man who has emerged from it may profess the experience by using the limit-word of non-duality, but without any right to proclaim this as unity.

We, however, are resolved to tend with holy care the holy treasure of our actuality that has been given to us for

[7]Khandogya Upanishad, VIII. 11. 1-3.

this life and perhaps for no other life that might be closer to the truth.

In lived actuality there is no unity of being. Actuality is to be found only in effective activity; strength and depth of the former only in that of the latter. "Inner" actuality, too, is only where there is reciprocal activity. The strongest and deepest actuality is to be found where everything enters into activity—the whole human being, without reserve, and the all-embracing god; the unified I and the boundless You.

The unified I: for (as I have said earlier) the unification of the soul occurs in lived actuality—the concentration of all forces into the core, the decisive moment of man. But unlike that immersion, this does not entail ignoring the actual person. Immersion wants to preserve only what is "pure," essential, and enduring, while stripping away everything else; the concentration of which I speak does not consider our instincts as too impure, the sensuous as too peripheral, or our emotions[8] as too fleeting—everything must be included and integrated. What is wanted is not the abstracted self but the whole, undiminished man. This concentration aims at and is actuality.

The doctrine of immersion demands and promises penetration into the thinking One, "that by which this world is thought," the pure subject. But in lived actuality no one thinks without something being thought; rather is that which thinks as dependent on that which is thought as vice versa. A subject that annuls the object to rise above it annuls its own actuality. A thinking subject by itself exists —in thought, as the product and object of thought, as a limit-concept that lacks all imaginable content; also in the anticipatory determination of death for which one may also substitute its metaphor, that deep sleep which is virtu-

[8]*das Gemüthafte:* Buber in March 1937: "emotions."

ally no less impenetrable; and finally in the assertions of a doctrine concerning a state of immersion that resembles such deep sleep and is essentially without consciousness and without memory. These are the supreme excesses of It-language. One has to respect its sublime power to ignore while at the same time recognizing it as something that can at most be an object of living experience but that cannot be lived.

Buddha, the "Perfected" and perfecter, asserts not. He refuses to claim that unity exists or does not exist; that he who has passed through all the trials of immersion will persist in unity after death or that he will not persist in it. This refusal, this "noble silence," has been explained in two ways. Theoretically: because perfection is said to elude the categories of thought and assertion. Practically: because the unveiling of such truths would not aid salvation.[9] In truth both explanations belong together: whoever treats being as the object of an assertion, pulls it down into division,[1] into the antitheses of the It-world—in which there is no salvation. "When, O monk, the view prevails that soul and body are identical, there is no salvation; when, O monk, the view prevails that the soul is one and the body another, then also there is no salvation." In the envisaged mystery, even as in lived actuality, neither "thus it is" nor "thus it is not" prevails, neither being nor not-being, but rather thus-and-otherwise, being and not-being, the indissoluble. To confront the undivided[2] mystery undivided, that is the primal condition of salvation.[3] That the Buddha belongs to those who recognized this, is certain. Like all true teachers, he wishes to teach not a view but the

[9]Throughout this passage *Heilsleben* (literally, life of salvation) has been rendered simply as salvation.
[1] *Schiedlichkeit* is a coinage and more eccentric than division.
[2] *Unschiedlich(en)* is again more eccentric than undivided.
[3]Here, for the first time in this passage, Buber uses *Heil(s)*.

way. He contests only one assertion, that of the "fools"
who say that there is no acting, no deed, no strength: we
can go the way. He risks only one assertion, the decisive
one: "There is, O monks, what is Unborn, Unbecome,
Uncreated, Unformed"; if that were not, there would be
no goal; this *is*, the way has a goal.

So far we may follow the Buddha, faithful to the truth
of our encounter; going further would involve a betrayal
of the actuality of our own life. For according to the truth
and actuality that we do not fetch from our own depths but
that has been inspired in us and apportioned to us, we
know: if this is merely one of the goals, then it cannot be
ours; and if it is *the* goal, then it has been misnamed. And:
if it is one of the goals, then the path may lead all the way
to it; if it is *the* goal, then the path merely leads closer to
it.

The goal was for the Buddha "the annulment of suffering," which is to say, of becoming and passing away—the
salvation from the wheel of rebirth. "Henceforth there is
no recurrence" was to be the formula for those who had
liberated themselves from the desire for existence and thus
from the compulsion to become again ceaselessly. We do
not know whether there is a recurrence; the line of this
dimension of time in which we live we do not extend
beyond this life; and we do not try to uncover what will
reveal itself to us in its own time and law. But if we did
know that there was recurrence, then we should not seek
to escape from it: we should desire not crude existence but
the chance to speak in every existence, in its appropriate
manner and language, the eternal I of the destructible and
the eternal You of the indestructible.[4]

[4] *das ewige Ich des Vergänglichen und das ewige Du des Unvergänglichen.*
Vergänglich is what passes away, and the adjective could also be rendered by "transitory" or "perishable." Here the adjective is made
into a noun that could be masculine and personal or neuter and im-

Whether the Buddha leads men to the goal of redemption from having to recur, we do not know. Certainly he leads to an intermediate goal that concerns us, too: the unification of the soul. But he leads there not only, as is necessary, away from the "jungle of opinions," but also away from the "deception of forms"—which for us is no deception but (in spite of all the paradoxes of intuition that make for subjectivity but *for us simply belong to it*) the reliable world. His path, too, is a way of ignoring something, and when he bids us become aware of the processes in our body, what he means is almost the opposite of our sense-assured insight into the body. Nor does he lead the unified being further to that supreme You-saying that is open to it. His inmost decision seems to aim at the annulment of the ability to say You.

The Buddha knows saying You to man—that is clear from his greatly superior, but also greatly direct, intercourse with his disciples—but he does not teach it: to this love, which means "boundless inclusion in the heart of all that has become," the simple confrontation of being by being remains alien. In the depths of his silence he certainly knows, too, the You-saying to the primal ground, transcending all the "gods" whom he treats like disciples; it was from a relational process that became substance that his deed came, clearly as an answer to the You; but of this he remains silent.

personal. The whole construction is remote from ordinary language. The writer seems less concerned with precise denotation than with rich connotations and associations.
A German reader may well feel reminded of the final Chorus in Goethe's *Faust:* "What is destructible / Is but a metaphor . . ." Buber himself must also have known Nietzsche's poem "To Goethe" whieh begins: "The indestructible / is but your metaphor . . ." *Gleichnis,* the word used in these lines by Goethe and Nietzsche, recurs frequently in these pages and has always been translated as "metaphor."

His following among the nations, however, "the great vehicle,"[5] denied him gloriously. They addressed the eternal You of man—using the name of the Buddha. And they expect as the coming Buddha, the last one of his eon, him that shall fulfill love.

All doctrines of immersion are based on the gigantic delusion of a human spirit bent back into itself—the delusion that spirit occurs in man. In truth it occurs from man —between man and what he is not.[6] As the spirit bent back into itself renounces this sense, this sense of relation, he must draw into man that which is not man, he must psychologize[7] world and God. This is the psychical delusion[8] of the spirit.

"I proclaim, friend," says the Buddha, "that in this fathom-sized, feeling-afflicted ascetic's body dwell the world and the origin of the world and the annulment of the world and the path that leads to the annulment of the world."

That is true, but ultimately it is no longer true.

Certainly, the world dwells in me as a notion,[9] just as I dwell in it as a thing. But that does not mean that it is in me, just as I am not in it. The world and I include each other reciprocally.[1] This contradiction for thought, which inheres in the It-relation, is annulled by the You-relation

[5]The literal meaning of Mahayana, the Buddhism of Nepal, Tibet, China, Korea, and Japan.
[6]These locutions are as extraordinary in German as they are in English.
[7]*verseelen:* a coinage.
[8]*Seelenwahn:* another coinage.
[9]. . . *die Welt in mir als Vorstellung:* an allusion to Schopenhauer's main work, *Die Welt als Wille und Vorstellung,* translated as *The World as Will and Representation* (or *Idea*). For a detailed discussion of *Vorstellung,* including reasons for translating it as notion, see Kaufmann's *Hegel,* section 34.
[1]*sind wechselseitig einbezogen:* Buber in March 1937 said he meant that "The world and I are mutually included one in the other."

which detaches me from the world in order to relate me to it.

The self-sense, that which cannot be included in the world, I carry in myself. The being-sense, that which cannot be included in any notion, the world carries in itself. But this is not a thinkable "will"[2] but the whole worldliness of the world, just as the former is not a "knowing subject" but the whole I-likeness[3] of the I. No further "reduction" is valid here: whoever does not honor the ultimate unities thwarts the sense that is only comprehensible but not conceptual.[4]

The origin of the world and the annulment of the world are not in me; neither are they outside me; they simply are not—they always occur, and their occurrence is also connected with me, with my life, my decision, my work, my service, and also depends on me, on my life, my decision, my work, and my service. But what it depends on is not whether I "affirm" or "negate" the world in my soul, but how I let the attitude of my soul toward the world come to life, life that affects the world, actual life—and in actual life paths coming from very different attitudes of the soul can cross.[5] But whoever merely has a living "experience" of his attitude and retains it in his soul may be as thoughtful as can be, he is worldless—and all the games, arts, intoxications, enthusiasms, and mysteries that happen within him do not touch the world's skin. As long as one attains redemption only in his self, he cannot do any good or harm

[2]As Schopenhauer taught.
[3]*Ichhaftigkeit.*
[4]*den nur begreifbaren, nicht begrifflichen Sinn.*
[5]*können die Wege von sehr verschiednen Seelenhaltungen aus einander kreuzen.* In the original edition of 1923 *auseinander* was printed as one word, which would make the interpretation in the text above impossible; but this was a printer's error: Buber's manuscript leaves no doubt about that and moreover had originally *begegnen* instead of *kreuzen,* which shows that *aus* goes with *von* and not with *einander.*

to the world; he does not concern it. Only he that believes in the world achieves contact with it; and if he commits himself he also cannot remain godless. Let us love the actual world that never wishes to be annulled, but love it in all its terror, but dare to embrace it with our spirit's arms —and our hands encounter the hands that hold it.

I know nothing of a "world" and of "worldly life" that separate us from God. What is designated that way is life with an alienated It-world, the life of experience and use. Whoever goes forth in truth to the world, goes forth to God. Concentration and going forth, both in truth, the one-and-the-other which is the One, are what is needful.

God embraces but is not the universe;[6] just so, God embraces but is not my self. On account of this which cannot be spoken about, I can say in my language, as all can say in theirs: You. For the sake of this there are I and You, there is dialogue, there is language, and spirit whose primal deed language is, and there is, in eternity, the word.

*

Man's "religious" situation, existence in the presence, is marked by its essential and indissoluble antinomies. That these antinomies are indissoluble constitutes their very essence. Whoever affirms the thesis and repudiates the antithesis violates the sense of the situation. Whoever tries to think a synthesis destroys the sense of the situation. Whoever strives to relativize the antinomies annuls the sense of the situation. Whoever would settle the conflict between antinomies by some means short of his own life transgresses against the sense of the situation. It is the sense of the situation that it is to be lived in all its antinomies—only

[6] *das All* corresponds to the Brahma of the Upanishads, and the self to Atman.

lived—and lived ever again, ever anew, unpredictably, without any possibility of anticipation or prescription.

A comparison of the religious and the philosophical antinomy will make this clearer. Kant can relativize the philosophical conflict of freedom and necessity by relegating the latter to the world of appearance and the former to that of being, so that the two positions no longer really oppose one another but rather get along with one another as well as do the two worlds in which each is valid. But when I mean freedom and necessity not in worlds that are thought of but in the actuality in which I stand before God; when I know, "I have been surrendered" and know at the same time, "It depends on me," then I may not try to escape from the paradox I have to live by relegating the irreconcilable propositions to two separate realms; neither may I seek the aid of some theological artifice to attain some conceptual reconciliation: I must take it upon myself to live both in one, and lived both are one.

*

The eyes of an animal have the capacity of a great language. Independent, without any need of the assistance of sounds and gestures, most eloquent when they rest entirely in their glance, they express the mystery in its natural captivity, that is, in the anxiety of becoming.[7] This state of the mystery is known only to the animal, which alone can open it up to us—for this state can only be opened up and not revealed. The language in which this is accomplished is what it says: anxiety—the stirring of the creature between the realms of plantlike security and spiritual risk. This language is the stammering of nature under the initial grasp of spirit, before language yields to spirit's cosmic risk

[7] *Bangigkeit des Werdens.*

which we call man. But no speech will ever repeat what the stammer is able to communicate.

I sometimes look into the eyes of a house cat. The domesticated animal has not by any means received the gift of the truly "eloquent" glance from *us*, as a human conceit suggests sometimes; what it has from us is only the ability—purchased with the loss of its elementary natural-ness—to turn this glance upon us brutes.[8] In this process some mixture of surprise and question has come into it, into its dawn and even its rise—and this was surely wholly absent from the original glance, for all its anxiety. Undeni-ably, this cat began its glance by asking me with a glance that was ignited by the breath of my glance: "Can it be that you mean me? Do you actually want that I should not merely do tricks for you? Do I concern you? Am I there for you? Am I there? What is that coming from you? What is that around me? What is it about me? What is that?!" ("I" is here a paraphrase of a word of I-less self-reference that we lack. "That" represents the flood of man's glance in the entire actuality of its power to relate.) There the glance of the animal, the language of anxiety, had risen hugely—and set almost at once. My glance, to be sure, endured longer; but it no longer retained the flood of man's glance.

That rotation of the world's axis which introduced the relational process had been succeeded almost immediately by the next, which concludes it. Just now the It-world had surrounded the animal and me, then the You-world ra-diated from the ground for the length of one glance, and now its light has died back into the It-world.

It is for the sake of the language of this barely percepti-ble rising and setting of the spirit sun that I relate this

[8] *uns Untieren* could mean "us non-animals"; but *Untier* almost invaria-bly means monster, beast, brute.

minute occurrence that happened to me more than once.
No other event has made me so deeply aware of the
evanescent actuality in all relationships to other beings, the
sublime melancholy of our lot, the fated lapse into It of
every single You. For usually a day, albeit brief, separated
the morning and evening of the event; but here morning
and evening merged cruelly, the bright You appeared and
vanished: had the burden of the It-world really been taken
from the animal and me for the length of one glance? At
least I could still remember it, while the animal had sunk
again from its stammering glance into speechless anxiety,
almost devoid of memory.

How powerful is the continuum of the It-world, and
how tender the manifestations of the You!

There is so much that can never break through the crust
of thinghood! O fragment of mica,[9] it was while contem-

---

[9] *O Glimmerstück:* It is doubtful that most German readers get Buber's
meaning, but in March 1937 he wrote his first translator that he meant
"das Mineral, das englisch mica *heisst; also:* fragment of mica."
Cf. Buber's earlier book, *Daniel* (1913), 148 f.: "I walked on the road one
dim morning, saw a piece of mica lying there, picked it up, and looked
at it for a long time. The day was no longer dim: so much light was
caught by the stone. And suddenly, as I looked away, I realized that
while looking at it I had known nothing of "object" and "subject"; as
I looked, the piece of mica and "I" had been one; as I looked, I had tasted
unity. I looked at it again, but unity did not return. Then something
flamed up inside me as if I were about to create. I closed my eyes, I
concentrated my strength, I entered into an association with my object,
I raised the piece of mica into the realm of that which has being. And
then, Lucas, only then did I feel: *I;* only then was I. He that had looked
had not yet been I; only this, this being in association [*dieses Verbund-
ene*] bore the name like a crown. Now I felt about this former unity as
a marble image might feel about the block from which it has been
carved: it was the undifferentiated, while I was the unification. As yet
I did not understand myself . . .
"True unity cannot be found, it can only be done."
And a few pages later: "Can the low tide say I? Or the high tide? But
attribute a spirit to the sea and include in it the unity of low tide and
high tide: that could say I.
"The piece of mica couldn't; the man looking at it couldn't; and the
undifferentiated state of the initial look was mere material. But once

plating you that I first understood that I is not something
"in me"—yet I was associated with you only in myself; it
was only in me, not between you and me that it happened
that time. But when something does emerge from among
things, something living, and becomes a being for me, and
comes to me, near and eloquent, how unavoidably briefly
it is for me nothing but You! It is not the relationship that
necessarily wanes, but the actuality of its directness. Love
itself cannot abide in a direct relation; it endures, but in
the alternation of actuality and latency. Every You
in the world is compelled by its nature to become a
thing for us or at least to enter again and again into thinghood.

Only in one relationship, the all-embracing one, is even
latency actuality. Only one You never ceases, in accordance with its nature to be You for us. To be sure, whoever
knows God also knows God's remoteness and the agony
of drought upon a frightened heart, but not the loss of
presence. Only we are not always there.

The lover of the *Vita Nuova* is right in usually saying
Ella and only occasionally *Voi*. The visionary of the
Paradiso speaks inauthentically, from poetic constraint,
when he says *Colui*, and he knows it.[1] Whether one speaks
of God as He or It, this is never more than allegory. But

their tension had taken form, that which had become associated could.
"What we ordinarily call I is a point of departure and makeshift—a
grammatical fact. But the I of the tension is a work and actuality [*Werk
und Wirklichkeit*]" (151 f.).
The book ends less than two pages after that—and many of its themes
are taken up again and developed further in *Ich und Du. Daniel* consists
of five short dialogues, each devoted to one key term, and four of the
five terms recur in the later work: *Richtung* (direction), *Wirklichkeit*
(actuality), *Sinn* (sense), and *Einheit* (unity). *Polarität* (polarity) has been
given such a new twist that the word does not reappear in *Ich und Du*
—except for the Afterword, in which we encounter bipolarity.
[1]The three Italian words may be rendered as she, you, and that one.
Buber writes *Vita Nova*. The lover and visionary is, of course, Dante.

when we say You to him, the unbroken truth of the world has been made word by mortal sense.

*

Every actual relationship in the world is exclusive; the other breaks into it to avenge its exclusion. Solely in the relation to God are unconditional exclusiveness and unconditional inclusiveness one in which the universe is comprehended.

Every actual relationship in the world rests upon individuation: that is its delight, for only thus is mutual recognition of those who are different granted—and that is its boundary, for thus is perfect recognition and being recognized denied. But in the perfect relationship my You embraces my self without being it; my limited recognition is merged into a boundless being-recognized.

Every actual relationship in the world alternates between actuality and latency; every individual You must disappear into the chrysalis of the It in order to grow wings again. In the pure relationship, however, latency is merely actuality drawing a deep breath during which the You remains present. The eternal You is You by its very nature;[2] only *our* nature forces us to draw it into the It-world and It-speech.

*

The It-world coheres in space and time.

The You-world does not cohere in either.

It coheres in the center in which the extended lines of relationships intersect: in the eternal You.

In the great privilege of the pure relationship the privi-

[2] The meaning is not so clear in the original, but Buber explained in March 1937 that this was what he meant.

leges of the It-world are annulled. By virtue of it the You-world is continuous: the isolated moments of relationships join for a world life of association.[3] By virtue of it the You-world has the power to give form: the spirit can permeate the It-world and change it. By virtue of it we are not abandoned to the alienation of the world and the deactualization of the I, nor are we overpowered by phantoms.[4] Return signifies the re-cognition of the center, turning back to it again. In this essential deed man's buried power to relate is resurrected, the wave of all relational spheres surges up in a living flood and renews our world.

Perhaps not only ours. Dimly we apprehend this double movement—that turning away from the primal ground by virtue of which the universe preserves itself in its becoming, and that turning toward the primal ground by virtue of which the universe redeems itself in being—as the metacosmic primal form of duality that inheres in the world as a whole in its relation to that which is not world, and whose human form is the duality of attitudes, of basic words, and of the two aspects of the world.[5] Both movements are unfolded fatefully in time and enclosed, as by grace, in the timeless creation that, incomprehensibly, is at once release and preservation, at once bond and liberation. Our knowledge of duality is reduced to silence by the paradox of the primal mystery.

*

Three are the spheres in which the world of relation is built.[6]

[3] *verbinden sich zu einem Weltleben der Verbundenheit.*
[4] *das Gespenstische.*
[5] In the original, this is one of the most baffling sentences in the book and has to be construed painstakingly to be understood.
[6] This passage is very similar to the ninth section of the First Part; see pp. 56ff.

The first: life with nature, where the relation sticks to the threshold of language.

The second: life with men, where it enters language.

The third: life with spiritual beings, where it lacks but creates language.

In every sphere, in every relational act, through everything that becomes present to us, we gaze toward the train of the eternal You; in each we perceive a breath of it; in every You we address the eternal You, in every sphere according to its manner. All spheres are included in it, while it is included in none.

Through all of them shines the one presence.

But we can take each out of the presence.

Out of life with nature we can take the "physical" world, that of consistency; out of life with men, the "psychical" world, that of affectability; out of life with spiritual beings, the "noetic" world, that of validity. Now they have been deprived of their transparency and thus of sense; each has become usable and murky, and remains murky even if we endow it with shining names: cosmos, eros, logos. For in truth there is a cosmos for man only when the universe becomes a home for him with a holy hearth where he sacrifices; and there is eros for him only when beings become for him images of the eternal, and community with them becomes revelation; and there is logos for him only when he addresses the mystery with works and service of the spirit.

The demanding silence of forms, the loving speech of human beings, the eloquent muteness of creatures—all of these are gateways into the presence of the word.

But when the perfect encounter is to occur, the gates are unified into the one gate of actual life, and you no longer know through which one you have entered.

*

Of these three spheres one is distinguished: life with men. Here language is perfected as a sequence and becomes speech and reply. Only here does the word, formed in language, encounter its reply. Only here does the basic word go back and forth in the same shape; that of the address and that of the reply are alive in the same tongue; I and You do not only stand in a relationship but also in firm honesty.[7] The moments of relation are joined here, and only here, through the element of language in which they are immersed. Here that which confronts us has developed the full actuality of the You. Here alone beholding and being beheld, recognizing and being recognized, loving and being loved exist as an actuality that cannot be lost.

This is the main portal into whose inclusive opening the two side portals lead.

"When a man is intimate[8] with his wife, the longing of the eternal hills wafts about them."

The relation to a human being is the proper metaphor for the relation to God—as genuine address is here accorded a genuine answer. But in God's answer all, the All,[9] reveals itself as language.

*

—But isn't solitude, too, a portal? Does it not happen sometimes in the stillest lonesomeness that we unexpectedly behold? Cannot intercourse with oneself change mysteriously into intercourse with mystery? Indeed, is not

[7] *"Redlichkeit"* means honesty but has the same root as *reden* (speak) and *Rede* (speech).
[8] "Intimate" (*innig*) was added in 1957.
[9] *alles, das All:* elsewhere, *das All* has been translated as "the universe."

only he that is no longer attached to any being worthy of confronting being? "Come, lonesome one to the lonesome," Simeon, the New Theologian,[1] addresses his God.

—There are two kinds of lonesomeness, depending on what it turns away from. If lonesomeness means detaching oneself from experiencing and using things, then this is always required to achieve any act of relation, not only the supreme one. But if lonesomeness means the absence of relation: if other beings have forsaken us after we had spoken the true You to them, we will be accepted by God; but not if we ourselves have forsaken other beings. Only he that is full of covetousness to use them is *attached* to some of them; he that lives in the strength of the presence can only be associated with them. The latter, however— he alone is ready for God. For he alone counters God's actuality with a human actuality.

And again there are two kinds of lonesomeness, depending on what it turns to. If lonesomeness is the place of purification which even the associate needs before he enters the holy of holies, but which he also needs in the midst of his trials, between his unavoidable failures and his ascent to prove himself[2]—that is how we are constituted. But if it is the castle of separation where man conducts a dialogue with himself, not in order to test himself and master himself for what awaits him but in his enjoyment of the configuration of his own soul—that is the spirit's lapse into mere spirituality. And this becomes truly abysmal when self-deception reaches the point where one thinks that one has God within and speaks to him. But as surely as God embraces us and dwells in us, we never have him within.

[1] A mystic of the Eastern Church who lived around A.D. 1000.
[2] Buber in March 1937: "*Nicht* renunciation; *Versagen ist hier* failing. *Nicht* confirmation; *Bewährung:* proving true."

And we speak to him only when all speech has ceased within.

*

A modern philosopher supposes that every man believes of necessity either in God or in "idols"—which is to say, some finite good, such as his nation, his art, power, knowledge, the acquisition of money, the "ever repeated triumph with women"—some good that has become an absolute value for him, taking its place between him and God; and if only one proves to a man the conditionality of this good, thus "smashing" the idol, then the diverted religious act would all by itself return to its proper object.[3]

This view presupposes that man's relation to the finite goods that he "idolizes" is essentially the same as his relationship to God, as if only the object were different: only

[3] Max Scheler, *Vom Ewigen im Menschen* (Berlin 1921; Engl. tr., *On the Eternal in Man*, London 1960) contains a section entitled "The religious act is performed of necessity by every human being." Here we find not only the position criticized by Buber but also the phrases he quotes. The book was written during the brief period when Scheler was a convert to Roman Catholicism. Soon he abandoned Catholicism and theism, but in his *Philosophische Weltanschauung* (1929; he died in 1928) the point about "idolatry" and smashing idols is repeated in the opening pages. In the English-speaking world the position attacked by Buber was made familiar by Tillich who kept restating it in his late works, after World War II—without giving credit to Scheler and without meeting Buber's criticism. Although Tillich's remarks about idolatry attracted a good deal of attention, I have not found any comparisons with the relevant passages in Scheler or Buber. And although *I and Thou* is a classic, not one of the scholars I asked knew whom Buber had had in mind; only Professor Hugo Bergman, Buber's contemporary and friend, recalled that the "modern philosopher" was Max Scheler.

For Buber's interest in Scheler, see especially *Werke*, Vol. I, pp. 380ff. (*Between Man and Man*, pp. 181ff.), where idolatry is not discussed. Tillich's books contain occasional references to Scheler, but not to his discussions of idolatry and the ground of being.

in that case could the mere substitution of the proper object for the wrong one save the man who has gone wrong. But a man's relation to the "particular something" that arrogates the supreme throne of his life's values, pushing eternity aside, is always directed toward the experience and use of an It, a thing, an object of enjoyment. For only this kind of relation can bar the view to God, by interposing the impenetrable It-world; the relationship that says You always opens it up again. Whoever is dominated by the idol whom he wants to acquire, have, and hold, possessed by his desire to possess, can find a way to God only by returning, which involves a change not only of the goal but also of the kind of movement. One can heal the possessed only by awakening and educating him to association, not by directing his possession toward God. If a man remains in the state of possession, what does it mean that he no longer invokes the name of a demon or of a being that is for him distorted demonically, but that of God? It means that he blasphemes. It is blasphemy when a man whose idol has fallen down behind the altar desires to offer to God the unholy sacrifice that is piled up on the desecrated altar.

When a man loves a woman so that her life is present in his own, the You of her eyes allows him to gaze into a ray of the eternal You. But if a man lusts after the "ever repeated triumph"—you want to dangle before his lust a phantom of the eternal? If one serves a people in a fire kindled by immeasurable fate—if one is willing to devote oneself to it, one means God. But if the nation is for him an idol to which he desires to subjugate everything because in its image he extols his own—do you fancy[4] that you only have to spoil the nation for him and he will then see the truth? And what is it supposed to mean that a man treats

[4] *wähnt.* Until 1957: *meint* (suppose).

money, which is un-being[5] incarnate, "as if it were God"?
What does the voluptuous delight of rapacity and hoarding
have in common with the joy over the presence of that
which is present? Can mammon's slave say You to money?
And what could God be to him if he does not know how
to say You? He cannot serve two masters[6]—not even one
after the other; he must first learn to serve differently.

Whoever has been converted by substitution, now "has"
a phantom that he calls God. God, however, the eternal
presence, cannot be had. Woe unto the possessed who
fancy that they possess God!

*

People speak of the "religious man" as one who can
dispense with all relationships to the world and to beings
because the social stage that is allegedly determined from
outside is supposed to have been transcended here by a
force that works entirely from within. But two basically
different notions are confused when people use the concept of the social: the community built of relation and the
amassing of human units that have no relation to one another—the palpable manifestation of modern man's lack of
relation. The bright edifice of community, however, for
which one can be liberated even from the dungeon of
"sociability,"[7] is the work of the same force that is alive in
the relation between man and God. But this is not one
relation among others; it is the universal relation[8] into
which all rivers pour without drying up for that reason. Sea
and rivers—who would make bold to separate here and

[5] *Unwesen* can also mean monster, disorder.
[6] "No one can serve two masters . . . You cannot serve God and mammon" (Matthew 6:24; cf. Luke 16:13).
[7] *"Sozialität."*
[8] *Allbeziehung.*

define limits? There is only the one flood from I to You, ever more infinite, the one boundless flood of actual life. One cannot divide one's life between an actual relationship to God and an inactual I-It relationship to the world—praying to God in truth and utilizing the world. Whoever knows the world as something to be utilized knows God the same way. His prayers are a way of unburdening himself—and fall into the ears of the void. He—and not the "atheist" who from the night and longing of his garret window[9] addresses the nameless—is godless.

It is said further that the "religious" man steps before God as one who is single, solitary, and detached insofar as he has also transcended the stage of the "ethical" man who still dwells in duty and obligation to the world. The latter is said to be still burdened with responsibility for the actions of agents because he is wholly determined by the tension between is and ought, and into the unbridgeable gap between both he throws, full of grotesquely hopeless sacrificial courage, piece upon piece of his heart. The "religious" man is supposed to have transcended this tension between world and God; the commandment for him is to leave behind the restlessness of responsibility and of making demands on himself; for him there is no longer any room for a will of one's own, he accepts his place in the Plan;[1] any ought is dissolved in unconditional being, and the world, while still persisting, has lost its validity; one still has to do one's share in it but, as it were, without obligation, in the perspective of the nullity of all activity. Thus men fancy[2] that God has created his world to be an illusion and his man to reel. Of course, whoever steps

[9] *Kammerfensters.* Buber explained in March 1937 that he was thinking of a *Dachkammer* and proposed the English words, "of his garret-window," adding (in German): "it is a poor student who lives in a garret; at night he opens the window and looks out into the infinite dark."
[1] *das in die Fügung Gefügt-sein.*
[2] Until 1957: *meinen* (suppose).

before the countenance has soared way beyond duty and obligation—but not because he has moved away from the world; rather because he has come truly close to it. Duties and obligations one has only toward the stranger: toward one's intimates one is kind and loving. When a man steps before the countenance, the world becomes wholly present to him for the first time in the fullness of the presence, illuminated by eternity, and he can say You in one word to the being of all beings.[3] There is no longer any tension between world and God but only the one actuality. He is not rid of responsibility: for the pains of the finite version that explores effects he has exchanged the momentum of the infinite kind, the power of loving responsibility for the whole unexplorable course of the world, the deep inclusion in the world before the countenance of God. Ethical judgments, to be sure, he has left behind forever: "evil" men are for him merely those commended to him for a deeper responsibility, those more in need of love; but decisions he must continue to make in the depths of spontaneity unto death—calmly deciding ever again in favor of right action. Thus action is not null: it is intended, it is commanded, it is needed, it belongs to the creation; but this action no longer imposes itself upon the world, it grows upon it as if it were non-action.

*

What is it that is eternal: the primal phenomenon, present in the here and now, of what we call revelation? It is man's emerging from the moment of the supreme encounter, being no longer the same as he was when entering into it. The moment of encounter is not a "living experience"[4]

[3] *zur Wesenheit aller Wesen.*
[4] *"Erlebnis."*

that stirs in the receptive soul and blissfully rounds itself
out: something happens to man. At times it is like feeling
a breath and at times like a wrestling match; no matter:
something happens. The man who steps out of the essential act of pure relation has something More in his being,
something new has grown there of which he did not know
before and for whose origin he lacks any suitable words.
Whereever the scientific world orientation in its legitimate
desire for a causal chain without gaps may place the origin
of what is new here: for us, being concerned with the
actual contemplation of the actual, no subconscious and no
other psychic apparatus will do. Actually, we receive what
we did not have before, in such a manner that we know:
it has been given to us. In the language of the Bible: "Those
who wait for God will receive strength in exchange."[5] In
the language of Nietzsche who is still faithful to actuality in his report: "One accepts, one does not ask who
gives."[6]

Man receives, and what he receives is not a "content"
but a presence, a presence as strength. This presence and
strength includes three elements that are not separate but
may nevertheless be contemplated as three. First, the
whole abundance of actual reciprocity, of being admitted,
of being associated while one is altogether unable to indicate what that is like with which one is associated, nor does
association make life any easier for us—it makes life
heavier[7] but heavy with meaning. And this is second: the
inexpressible confirmation of meaning. It is guaranteed.
Nothing, nothing can henceforth be meaningless. The

[5]Isaish 40:31. "They who wait for the Lord shall renew their strength"
(RSV).
[6]*Ecce Homo*, in section 3 of the discussion of *Zarathustra*.
[7]*schwer* means hard or difficult as well as heavy, and here the former
would be much more idiomatic and preferable if it were not for the
recurrence of the word in the same sentence.

question about the meaning of life has vanished. But if it were still there, it would not require an answer. You do not know how to point to or define the meaning, you lack any formula or image for it, and yet it is more certain for you than the sensations of your senses. What could it intend with us, what does it desire from us, being revealed and surreptitious? It does not wish to be interpreted by us—for that we lack the ability—only to be done by us. This comes third: it is not the meaning of "another life" but that of this our life, not that of a "beyond" but of this our world, and it wants to be demonstrated by us in this life and this world. The meaning can be received but not experienced; it cannot be experienced, but it can be done; and this is what it intends with us. The guarantee does not wish to remain shut up within me, it wants to be born into the world by me. But even as the meaning itself cannot be transferred or expressed as a universally valid and generally acceptable piece of knowledge, putting it to the proof in action[8] cannot be handed on as a valid ought; it is not prescribed, not inscribed on a table that could be put up over everybody's head. The meaning we receive can be put to the proof in action only by each person in the uniqueness of his being and in the uniqueness of his life. No prescription can lead us to the encounter, and none leads from it. Only the acceptance of the presence is required to come to it or, in a new sense, to go from it. As we have nothing but a You on our lips when we enter the encounter, it is with this on our lips that we are released from it into the world.

That before which we live, that in which we live, that out of which and into which we live, the mystery—has remained what it was. It has become present for us, and through its presence it has made itself known to us as

[8]*seine Bewährung.*

salvation; we have "known" it, but we have no knowledge of it that might diminish or extenuate its mysteriousness. We have come close to God, but no closer to an unriddling, unveiling of being. We have felt salvation but no "solution."[9] We cannot go to others with what we have received, saying: This is what needs to be known, this is what needs to be done. We can only go and put to the proof in action. And even this is not what we "ought to" do: rather we can—we cannot do otherwise.

This is the eternal revelation which is present in the here and now. I neither know of nor believe in any revelation that is not the same in its primal phenomenon. I do not believe in God's naming himself or in God's defining himself before man. The word of revelation is: I am there as whoever I am there.[1] That which reveals is that which reveals. That which has being is there,[2] nothing more. The eternal source of strength flows, the eternal touch is waiting, the eternal voice sounds, nothing more.

*

By its very nature the eternal You cannot become an It; because by its very nature it cannot be placed within measure and limit, not even within the measure of the immeasurable and the limit of the unlimited; because by its very nature it cannot be grasped as a sum of qualities, not even as an infinite sum of qualities that have been raised to transcendence; because it is not to be found either in or

[9] *Erlösung . . . "Lösung."*
[1] *Ich bin da als der ich da bin.* Before 1957: *Ich bin der ich bin.* Both sentences represent attempts to translate the Hebrew *Ehyeh asher ehyey* in Exodus 3:14. For an interpretation and discussion of Buber's later translation see Kaufmann, *Critique of Religion and Philosophy,* section 89.
[2] *Das Seiende ist da.* Before 1957: *Das Seiende ist.* Again, the stress on being *there,* on being present, was added later.

outside the world; because it cannot be experienced; because it cannot be thought; because we transgress against it, against that which has being, if we say: "I believe that he is"—even "he" is still a metaphor, while "you" is not.

And yet we reduce the eternal You ever again to an It, to something, turning God into a thing, in accordance with our nature. Not capriciously. The history of God as a thing, the way of the God-thing through religion and its marginal forms,[3] through its illuminations and eclipses, the times when it heightened and when it destroyed life, the way from the living God and back to him again, the metamorphoses of the present, of embedment in forms,[4] of objectification, of conceptualization, dissolution, and renewal are one way, are *the* way.

The asserted knowledge and the posited action of the religions—whence do they come? The presence and strength of revelation (for all of them necessarily invoke some sort of revelation, whether verbal, natural, or psychic —there are, strictly speaking,[5] only revealed religions), the presence and strength that man received through revelation—how do they become a "content"?

The explanation has two levels. The exoteric, psychic level is known when man is considered by himself, apart from history. The esoteric, factual one, the primal phenomenon of religion, when we afterward place him in history again. Both belong together.

Man desires to have God; he desires to have God continually in space and time. He is loath to be satisfied with the inexpressible confirmation of the meaning; he wants to see it spread out as something that one can take out and

[3]Buber in March 1937 suggested: "and through the products" and "fringe?" But "its marginal forms" is closer to *ihre Randgebilde.*
[4]*Eingestaltung:* a coinage.
[5]The preceding two words were added in 1957.

handle again and again—a continuum unbroken in space
and time that insures life for him at every point and moment.

Life's rhythm of pure relation, the alternation of actuality and a latency in which only our strength to relate and
hence also the presence, but not the primal presence,
wanes, does not suffice man's thirst for continuity. He
thirsts for something spread out in time, for duration. Thus
God becomes an object of faith. Originally, faith fills the
temporal gaps between the acts of relation; gradually, it
becomes a substitute for these acts. The ever new movement of being through concentration and going forth is
supplanted by coming to rest in an It in which one has
faith. The trust-in-spite-of-all of the fighter who knows the
remoteness and nearness of God is transformed ever more
completely into the profiteer's assurance that nothing can
happen to him because he has the faith that there is One
who would not permit anything to happen to him.

The life-structure of the pure relation, the "lonesomeness" of the I before the You, the law that man, however
he may include the world in his encounter, can still go
forth only as a person to encounter God—all this also does
not satisfy man's thirst for continuity. He thirsts for something spread out in space, for the representation in which
the community of the faithful is united with its God. Thus
God becomes a cult object. The cult, too, originally supplements the acts of relation, by fitting the living prayer, the
immediate You-saying into a spatial context of great plastic
power and connecting it with the life of the senses. And
the cult, too, gradually becomes a substitute, as the personal prayer is no longer supported but rather pushed aside
by communal prayer; and as the essential deed simply does
not permit any rules, it is supplanted by devotions that
follow rules.

In truth, however, the pure relation can be built up into spatio-temporal continuity only by becoming embodied in the whole stuff of life. It cannot be preserved[6] but only put to the proof in action;[7] it can only be done, poured into life. Man can do justice to the relation to God that has been given to him only by actualizing God in the world in accordance with his ability and the measure of each day, daily. This is the only genuine guarantee of continuity. The genuine guarantee of duration is that the pure relation can be fulfilled as the beings become You, as they are elevated to the You, so that the holy basic word sounds through all of them. Thus the time of human life is formed into an abundance of actuality; and although human life cannot and ought not to overcome the It-relation, it then becomes so permeated by relation that this gains a radiant and penetrating constancy in it. The moments of supreme encounter are no mere flashes of lightning in the dark but like a rising moon in a clear starry night. And thus the genuine guarantee of spatial constancy consists in this that men's relations to their true You, being radii that lead from all I-points to the center, create a circle. Not the periphery, not the community comes first, but the radii, the common relation to the center. That alone assures the genuine existence of a community.

The anchoring of time in a relation-oriented life of salvation and the anchoring of space in a community unified by a common center: only when both of these come to be and only as long as both continue to be, a human cosmos comes to be and continues to be around the invisible altar, grasped in the spirit out of the world stuff of the eon.[8]

[6] *bewahrt.*
[7] *bewährt.*
[8] The word twice rendered by "anchoring" is *die Bindung*, which means "the binding" but could also mean, in appropriate contexts, cohesion or obligation. Here the meaning required by the context is a tying down,

The encounter with God does not come to man in order
that he may henceforth attend to God[9] but in order that
he may prove its meaning in action in the world. All revelation is a calling and a mission. But again and again man
shuns actualization and bends back toward the revealer: he
would rather attend to God than to the world. Now that
he has bent back, however, he is no longer confronted by
a You; he can do nothing but place a divine It in the realm
of things, believe that he knows about God as an It, and
talk about him. Even as the egomaniac does not live anything directly, whether it be a perception or an affection,
but reflects on his perceiving or affectionate I and thus
misses the truth of the process, thus the theomaniac (who,
incidentally, can get along very well with the egomaniac in the very same soul) will not let the gift take full
effect but reflects instead on that which gives, and misses
both.

When you are sent forth, God remains presence for you;
whoever walks in his mission always has God before him:
the more faithful the fulfillment, the stronger and more
constant the nearness. Of course, he cannot attend to[1] God

but not by way of fettering someone and robbing him of his freedom.
"Anchoring" would seem to capture Buber's meaning.
The two adjectives in the first part of the sentence are coinages: *bezie-
hungsgemässen* and *mittegeeinten;* literally: relation-according and cen-
ter-unified.
Where we now have "a human cosmos," earlier editions, until 1957,
had: "a limitlike, formlike human cosmos, a homelike, houselike world,
a world shelter for man."
The main problem with this kind of writing is that those who take it
seriously are led to devote their attention to what might be meant, and
the question is rarely asked whether what is meant is true, or what
grounds there might be for either believing or disputing it.
[9] *sich mit Gott befasse.*
[1] *befassen kann er sich freilich mit Gott nicht:* the mild irony of this remark
is reinforced by the overtones of *befassen.* Literally, *befassen* means
to touch all over. While *sich mit etwas befassen* (the idiom used both
here and earlier) means to attend to something or occupy oneself
with something, the reflexive *sich* (oneself) may also suggest, at

but he can converse with him. Bending back, on the other hand, turns God into an object. It appears to be a turning toward the primal ground, but belongs in truth to the world movement of turning away, even as the apparent turning away of those who fulfill their mission belongs in truth to the world movement of turning toward.

For the two basic metacosmic movements of the world —its expansion into its own being and returning to association [with God][2]—attain their supreme human form, the true spirit form of their struggle and conciliation, their mixture and separation,[3] in the history of man's relation to God. It is in the return that the word is born on earth; in spreading out it enters the chrysalis of religion; in a new return it is reborn[4] with new wings.

Not caprice is at work here, although the movement toward the It may at times go so far that it holds down the movement of going forth again to the You and threatens to suffocate it.

The powerful revelations invoked by the religions are essentially the same as the quiet one[5] that occurs every-

least subliminally, touching oneself all over with God.

[2]Buber in March 1937: *"besser nur* [better only]: reversal to connexion (*nämlich der Welt mit Gott*)." These two English nouns were used throughout the first translation. "Reversal" has many misleading connotations and lacks the absolutely crucial Biblical overtones of "return" (see pp. 35ff) and "connexion" is almost equally unfortunate. *Verbundenheit* is hard to translate, but we have seen that one of the paradigms is the relation of the embryo to the mother (see p. 76): hardly a connection—because our primary associations with "connect" are inorganic and artificial. Buber did not know English well enough at the time to realize any of this. Nor could the translation of key terms that recur frequently throughout the book be changed in page proof. Buber's parenthetical gloss has led me to add two words in brackets in the text above.

[3]An allusion to fragment 17 of the pre-Socratic philosopher, Empedocles.

[4]Literally: it gives birth to itself.

[5]*der stillen:* cf. Nietzsche's *Zarathustra*, Part Two, "On Great Events": "the greatest events—those are not our loudest but our stillest hours."

where and at all times. The powerful revelations that stand
at the beginnings of great communities, at the turning-
points of human time, are nothing else than the eternal
revelation. But revelation does not pour into the world
through its recipient as if he were a funnel: it confers itself
upon him, it seizes his whole element in all of its suchness
and fuses with it. Even the man who is "mouth"[6] is precisely that and not a mouthpiece—not an instrument but
an organ, an autonomous, sounding organ; and to sound
means to modify sound.[7]

But there is a qualitative difference between historical
ages. There are times of ripening when the true element
of the human spirit, held down and buried, grows ready
underground with such pressure and such tension that it
merely waits to be touched by one who will touch it—and
then erupts. The revelation that then appears seizes the
whole ready element in all its suchness, recasts it and
produces a form, a new form of God in the world.

Ever new regions of the world and the spirit are thus
lifted up into form, called to divine form, in the course of
history, in the transformations of the human element. Ever
new spheres become the place of a theophany. It is not
man's own power that is at work here, neither is it merely
God passing through; it is a mixture of the divine and the
human. Whoever is sent forth in a revelation takes with
him in his eyes an image of God; however supra-sensible
it may be, he takes it along in the eyes of his spirit, in the
altogether not metaphorical but entirely real visual power[8]
of his spirit. The spirit also answers by beholding, a *form-
giving* beholding.[9] Although we on earth never behold

[6]A reference to Biblical Hebrew: see Exodus 4:16.
[7]*lauten heisst umlauten.*
[8]*realen Augenkraft.* Until 1957: *wirklichen Augenkraft.*
[9]bildendes *Schauen.*

God without world but only the world in God, by beholding we eternally form God's form.

Form is a mixture of You and It, too. In faith and cult it can freeze into an object; but from the gist of the relation that survives in it, it turns ever again into presence. God is near his forms as long as man does not remove them from him. In true prayer, cult and faith are unified and purified into living relation. That true prayer lives in religions testifies to their true life; as long as it lives in them, they live. Degeneration of religions means the degeneration of prayer in them: the relational power in them is buried more and more by objecthood; they find it ever more difficult to say You with their whole undivided being; and eventually man must leave their false security for the risk of the infinite in order to recover this ability, going from the community over which one sees only the vaulting dome of the temple and no longer the firmament into the ultimate solitude.[1] This impulse is most profoundly misunderstood when it is ascribed to "subjectivism": life before the countenance is life in the one actuality, the only true *"objectivum"*; and the man that goes forth desires to find refuge in that which has true being, before the merely apparent, illusory *objectivum* that he flees has disturbed his truth. Subjectivism is psychologization[2] while objectivism is reification of God; one a false fixation, the other a false liberation; both departures from the way of actuality, both attempts to find a substitute for it.

God is close to his forms when man does not remove them from him. But when the spreading movement of religion holds down the movement of return and removes the form from God, then the countenance of the form is

[1] *letzte Einsamkeit.*
[2] *Verseelung.*

extinguished, its lips are dead, its hands hang down, God does not know it any more, and the house of the world built around its altar, the human[3] cosmos, crumbles.

The decomposition of the word has occurred.

The word is present in revelation,[4] at work in the life of the form, and becomes valid in the dominion of the dead form.

Thus the path and counter-path of the eternal and eternally present word in history.

The ages in which the living word appears are those in which the association of I and world is renewed. The ages in which the active and effective word reigns are those in which the understanding between I and world is preserved; the ages in which the word becomes valid are those in which the deactualization, the alienation of I and world, the emergence of doom takes place—until the great shudder appears, the holding of breath in the dark, and the preparatory silence.

But the path is not a circle. It is the way. Doom becomes more oppressive in every new eon, and the return more explosive. And the theophany comes ever *closer*, it comes ever closer to the sphere *between beings*—comes closer to the realm that hides in our midst, in the between. History is a mysterious approach to closeness. Every spiral of its path leads us into deeper corruption and at the same time into more fundamental return. But the God-side of the event whose world-side is called return is called redemption.

[3] Before 1957: *geistgefasste* instead of *menschliche*.
[4] *Das Wort ist in der Offenbarung wesend* is utterly unidiomatic German, no less than the immediately preceding sentence.

AFTERWORD

In the first edition (1923) the page facing the last page of the text read:

> Conception of the work whose beginning is represented by this book: spring 1916; first complete draft of this book: fall 1919; final version: spring 1922.

IN OCTOBER 1957 Buber wrote the following Afterword for the second edition and omitted the three lines translated above.

Buber's footnotes will be found on page 183.

1

When I drafted the first sketch of this book (more than forty years ago), I felt impelled by an inner necessity. A vision that had afflicted me repeatedly since my youth but had always been dimmed again, had now achieved a constant clarity that was so evidently supra-personal that I soon knew that I ought to bear witness of it. Some time after I had earned the appropriate diction that permitted me to write the book in its definitive form,[1] it appeared that a good deal remained to be added—but in its own place, independently. Thus several shorter works came into being:[2] I found occasions to clarify the crucial vision by means of examples, to elaborate it by refuting objections, and to criticize views to which I owed something important but which had missed the central significance of the close association of the relation to God with the relation to one's fellow-men, which is my most essential concern. Later other discussions were added: of the anthropological foundations[3] and of the sociological implications.[4] Nevertheless it has become plain that by no means everything has been clarified sufficiently. Again and again readers have asked me what I might have meant here or there. For a long time I answered each individually, but gradually I saw that I could not do justice to these demands, and moreover I surely must not restrict the dialogical relationship to those readers who decide to speak up: perhaps some of those who remain silent deserve special consideration. Hence I resolved to answer publicly— first of all a few essential questions that are interrelated.

2

The first question might be formulated like this, with reasonable precision: The book speaks of our I-You relation not only to other men but also to beings and things that confront us in nature; what, then, constitutes the essential difference between the former and the latter? Or, still more precisely: if the I-You relation entails a reciprocity that embraces both the I and the You, how can the relationship to something in nature be understood in this fashion? Still more exactly: if we are to suppose that the beings and things in nature that we encounter as our You also grant us some sort of reciprocity, what is the character of this reciprocity, and what gives us the right to apply to it this basic concept?

Obviously, no sweeping answer can be given to this question. Instead of considering nature as a single whole, as we usually do, we must consider its different realms separately. Man once "tamed" animals, and he is still capable of bringing off this strange feat. He draws animals into his own sphere and moves them to accept him, a stranger, in an elementary manner and to accede to his ways. He obtains from them an often astonishing active response to his approach, to his address—and on the whole this response is the stronger and more direct, the more his relation amounts to a genuine You-saying. Not infrequently animals, like children, see through feigned tenderness. But outside the tamed circle, too, we occasionally encounter a similar contact between men and animals: some men have deep down in their being a potential partnership with animals—most often persons who are by no means "animalic" by nature but rather spiritual.

Animals are not twofold, like man: the twofoldness of the basic words I-You and I-It is alien to them although they can both turn toward another being and contemplate objects. We may say that in them twofoldness is latent. In the perspective of our You-saying to animals, we may call this sphere the threshold of mutuality.

It is altogether different with those realms of nature which lack the spontaneity that we share with animals. It is part of our concept of the plant that it cannot react to our actions upon it, that it cannot "reply." Yet this does not mean that we meet with no reciprocity at all in this sphere. We find here not the deed of posture of an individual being but a reciprocity of being itself—a reciprocity that has nothing except being.* The living wholeness and unity of a tree that denies itself to the eye, no matter how keen, of anyone who merely investigates, while it is manifest to those who say You, is present when *they* are present: they grant the tree the opportunity to manifest it, and now the tree that has being manifests it. Our habits of thought make it difficult for us to see that in such cases something is awakened by our attitude and flashes toward us from that which has being. What matters in this sphere is that we should do justice with an open mind to the actuality that opens up before us. This huge sphere that reaches from the stones to the stars I should like to designate as the pre-threshold, meaning the step that comes before the threshold.

3

Now we come to the questions posed by that sphere which might be called, sticking to the same sort of image, the "over-threshold" (*superliminare*),** meaning the lintel that is above the door: the sphere of the spirit.

*eine nichts als seiende.
**The Latin word is found in the Vulgate, e.g., Exodus 12:22.

Here, too, we must separate two realms, but the distinction cuts deeper than that within nature. On the one side is the spirit that has already entered the world and now can be perceived in it by means of our senses; on the other, the spirit that has not yet entered the world but is ready to do so and now becomes present to us. This distinction is founded on the fact that I can show you, more or less, my reader, the spiritual forms that have already entered the world, but not the others. The spiritual forms that are "at hand"* in our common world, no less than a thing or a natural being, I can point out to you as something actually or potentially accessible to you. But what has not yet entered the world I cannot point out to you. If I am asked here, too, in the case of this borderland, where one is supposed to find mutuality, I can only point indirectly to certain scarcely describable events in human life where spirit was encountered; and if this indirect procedure proves inadequate, nothing remains to me in the end but an appeal to the testimony of your own mysteries, my reader, which may be buried under debris but are presumably still accessible to you.

Let us now return to the first realm, to that which is "at hand." Here it is possible to adduce examples.

Let those who ask about this realm call to mind one of the traditional sayings of a master who died thousands of years ago. Let them try, as best they can, to receive this saying with their ears—as if the speaker had said it in their presence, addressing them. To this end they must turn with their whole being toward the speaker, who is not at hand, of the saying that is at hand. In other words, they must adopt toward the master who is dead and yet living

* *"vorhanden"*: because Buber keeps placing this word in quotes, it seems reasonable to preserve the image in translation; but in ordinary German the reference to the hand is not felt strongly, and *es ist vorhanden* does not greatly differ from "it exists." Heidegger makes much of the same term in *Sein und Zeit*.

that attitude which I call You-saying. If they succeed (and will and effort are not sufficient, but now and then it can be undertaken), they will hear a voice, perhaps none too clearly at first, that is identical with the voice that speaks to them through other genuine sayings of the same master. Now they will not be able any longer to do what they did as long as they treated the saying as an object: they will not be able to separate out content and rhythm; they receive nothing but the indivisible wholeness of something spoken.*

But here we are still dealing with a person and the manifestation of a person in his words. What I have in mind, however, is not limited to the continued presence of some personal existence in words. Hence I must supplement this account by pointing to an example in which there is no longer anything personal. As always, I choose an example that is associated with strong memories at least for some people. Take the Doric column, wherever it appears to a man who is able and ready to turn toward it. It confronted me for the first time out of a church wall in Syracuse into which it had been incorporated: secret primal measure presenting itself in such a simple form that nothing individual could be seen or enjoyed in it. What had to be achieved was what I was able to achieve: to confront and endure this spiritual form there that had passed through the mind and hand of man and become incarnate. Does the concept of mutuality disappear here? It merely merges into the darkness behind it—or it changes into a concrete state of affairs, coldly rejecting concepthood,** but bright and reliable.

From here we may also look across into that other realm where that which is "not at hand" belongs, the contact

*einer Gesprochenheit: as often, Buber coins an abstract noun—of a spokenness.
**die Begrifflichkeit.

with "spiritual beings," the *genesis* of word and form.

Spirit become word, spirit become form—whoever has been touched by the spirit and did not close himself off knows to some extent of the fundamental fact:* neither germinates and grows in the human world without having been sown; both issue from encounters with the other. Encounters not with Platonic Ideas (of which I have no direct knowledge whatever and which I am incapable of understanding as having any being) but with the spirit that blows around us and inspires us. Again I am reminded of the strange confession of Nietzsche who circumscribed the process of inspiration by saying that one accepts without asking who gives. That may be so—one does not ask, but one gives thanks.

Those who know the spirit's breath commit a transgression if they wish to gain power over the spirit or to determine its nature. But they are also unfaithful if they ascribe this gift to themselves.

4

Let us consider once more what has here been said about encounters with what is natural and with what is spiritual.

The question may be asked at this point whether we have any right to speak of a "reply" or "address" that comes from outside the sphere to which in our consideration of the orders of being we ascribe spontaneity and

das grundlegend Faktische sounds much more like a German philosopher than does the English translation. A "fundamental fact" has an air of concreteness, while Buber's phrase successfully avoids any imaginable content. Similarly, *in irgendeinem Grade* (in some degree or other) sounds vaguer than "to some extent"; and *weiss . . . um* is much more solemn than "knows . . . of" and suggests some profound mystery.

consciousness as if they were like a reply or address in the human world in which we live. Is what has here been said valid except as a "personalizing" metaphor? Are we not threatened by the dangers of a problematic "mysticism" that blurs the borderlines that are drawn, and necessarily have to be drawn, by all rational knowledge?

The clear and firm structure of the I-You relationship, familiar to anyone with a candid heart and the courage to stake it, is not mystical. To understand it we must sometimes step out of our habits of thought, but not out of the primal norms that determine man's thoughts about what is actual. Both in the realm of nature and in the realm of spirit—the spirit that lives on in sayings and works and the spirit that strives to become sayings and works—what acts on us may be understood as the action of what has being.

5

The next question no longer concerns the threshold, pre-threshold, and over-threshold of mutuality, but mutuality itself as the gate of entry into our existence.

People ask: What about the I-You relationship between men? Is this always entirely reciprocal? Could it be, is it permitted to be? Is it not, like everything human, subject to the limitations of our inadequacy, and is it not limited further by the inner laws that govern our life with one another?

The first of these two obstacles is surely familiar enough. Everything, from your own experience of looking day after day into the eyes of your "neighbor" who needs you after all but responds with the cold surprise of a stranger, to the melancholy of the holy men who repeatedly offered the great gift in vain—everything tells you that complete mutuality does not inhere in men's life with one another. It is a form of grace for which one must always be prepared but on which one can never count.

Yet there are also many I-You relationships that by their very nature may never unfold into complete mutuality if they are to remain faithful to their nature.

Elsewhere[5] I have characterized the relationship of a genuine educator to his pupil as being of this type. The teacher who wants to help the pupil to realize his best potentialities must intend him as this particular person, both in his potentiality and in his actuality. More precisely, he must know him not as a mere sum of qualities, aspirations, and inhibitions; he must apprehend him, and affirm him, as a whole. But this he can only do if he encounters him as a partner in a bipolar situation. And to give his influence unity and meaning, he must live through this situation in all its aspects not only from his own point of view but also from that of his partner. He must practice the kind of realization that I call embracing.* It is essential that he should awaken the I-You relationship in the pupil, too, who should intend and affirm his educator as this particular person; and yet the educational relationship could not endure if the pupil also practiced the art of embracing by living through the shared situation from the educator's point of view. Whether the I-You relationship comes to an end or assumes the altogether different character of a friendship, it becomes clear that the specifically educational relationship is incompatible with complete mutuality.

Another, no less instructive example of the normative limits of mutuality may be found in the relationship between a genuine psychotherapist and his patient. If he is

* *Umfassung.*

satisfied to "analyze" his patient—that is, to bring to light unconscious factors from his microcosm and to apply to a conscious project the energies that have been transformed by this emergence—he may successfully accomplish some repairs. At best, he may help a diffuse soul that is poor in structure to achieve at least some concentration and order. But he cannot absolve his true task, which is the regeneration of a stunted personal center. That can be brought off only by a man who grasps with the profound eye of a physician the buried, latent unity of the suffering soul, which can be done only if he enters as a partner into a person-to-person relationship, but never through the observation and investigation of an object. In order to promote coherently the liberation and actualization of this unity in a new situation in which the other person comes to terms with the world, the therapist, like the educator, must stand not only at his own pole of the bipolar relationship but also at the other pole, experiencing the effects of his own actions. Again the specific "healing" relationship would end as soon as the patient decided to practice the art of embracing and actually succeeded in experiencing events also from the doctor's point of view. Healing, like educating, requires that one lives in confrontation and is yet removed.

The most striking example of the normative limits of mutuality could probably be found in the work of those charged with the spiritual well-being of their congregation: here any attempt at embracing from the other side would violate the consecrated authenticity of the mission.

Every I-You relationship in a situation defined by the attempt of one partner to act on the other one so as to accomplish some goal depends on a mutuality that is condemned never to become complete.

6

In this context only one more question can be discussed, but this has to be taken up because it is incomparably the most important of all.

How—people ask—can the eternal You be at the same time exclusive and inclusive? How is it possible for man's You-relationship to God, which requires our unconditional turning toward God, without any distraction, nevertheless to embrace all the other I-You relationships of this man and to bring them, as it were, to God?

Note that the question is not about God but only about our relationship to him. And yet in order to be able to answer, I have to speak of him. For our relationship to him is as supra-contradictory as it is because he is as supra-contradictory as he is.

Of course, we shall speak only of what God is in his relationship to a human being. And even that can be said only in a paradox; or more precisely, by using a concept paradoxically; or still more precisely, by means of a paradoxical combination of a nominal concept with an adjective that contradicts the familiar content of the concept. The insistence on this contradiction must give way to the insight that thus, and only thus, the indispensable designation of this object by this concept can be justified. The content of the concept undergoes a revolutionary transformation and expansion, but that is true of every concept that, impelled by the actuality of faith, we take from the realm of immanence and apply to transcendence.

The designation of God as a person is indispensable for all who, like myself, do not mean a principle when they say "God," although mystics like Eckhart occasionally equate "Being" with him, and who, like myself, do not mean an idea when they say "God," although philosophers like

Plato could at times take him for one—all who, like myself, mean by "God" him that, whatever else he may be in addition, enters into a direct relationship to us human beings through creative, revelatory, and redemptive acts, and thus makes it possible for us to enter into a direct relationship to him. This ground and meaning of our existence establishes each time a mutuality of the kind that can obtain only between persons. The concept of personhood is, of course, utterly incapable of describing the nature of God; but it is permitted and necessary to say that God is *also* a person. If for once I were to translate what I mean into the language of a philosopher, Spinoza, I should have to say that of God's infinitely many attributes we human beings know not two, as Spinoza thought, but three: in addition to spiritlikeness—the source of what we call spirit—and naturelikeness, exemplified by what we know as nature, also thirdly the attribute of personlikeness.* From this last attribute I should then derive my own and all men's being persons, even as I should derive from the first two my own and all men's being spirit and being nature. And only this third attribute, personlikeness, could then be said to be known directly in its quality as an attribute.

But now the contradiction appears, appealing to the familiar content of the concept of a person. A person, it says, is by definition an independent individual and yet also relativized by the plurality of other independent individuals; and this, of course, could not be said of God. This contradiction is met by the paradoxical designation of God as the absolute person, that is one that cannot be relativized. It is as the absolute person that God enters into the

---

* *Geisthaftigkeit . . . Naturhaftigkeit . . . Personhaftigkeit.* These three coinages are highly abstract and elusive. The suffix *haftigkeit* has been discussed on p. 44f.

direct relationship to us. The contradiction must give way to this higher insight.

Now we may say that God carries his absoluteness into his relationship with man. Hence the man who turns toward him need not turn his back on any other I-You relationship: quite legitimately he brings them all to God and allows them to become transfigured "in the countenance of God."

One should beware altogether of understanding the conversation with God—the conversation of which I had to speak in this book and in almost all of my later books—as something that occurs merely apart from or above the everyday. God's address to man penetrates the events in all our lives and all the events in the world around us, everything biographical and everything historical, and turns it into instruction,* into demands for you and me. Event upon event, situation upon situation is enabled and empowered by this personal language to call upon the human person to endure and decide. Often we think that there is nothing to be heard as if we had not long ago plugged wax into our own ears.

The existence of mutuality between God and man cannot be proved any more than the existence of God. Anyone who dares nevertheless to speak of it bears witness and invokes the witness of those whom he addresses—present or future witness.

Jerusalem, October 1957

Martin Buber

* *Weisung* is Buber's translation of *Torah*. He entitled his version of the Pentateuch: *Die Fünf Bücher der Weisung*. But *ein Wegweiser* is a signpost that, literally, points the way. *Weisung* could also be rendered as "direction."

Buber's own footnotes for the AFTERWORD

1. It appeared in 1923.
2. *Zwiesprache* (1930). *Die Frage an den Einzelnen* (1936). *Über das Erzieherische* (1926). *Das Problem des Menschen* (Hebrew, 1943). All included in Martin Buber, *Werke*, vol. I: *Schriften zur Philosophie* (1962) [and in *Between Man and Man* (1937)].
3. *Urdistanz und Beziehung* (1950). Also in *Werke*, vol. I.
4. *Elemente des Zwischenmenschlichen* (1954). Also in *Werke*, vol. I.
5. *Über das Erzieherische*: see note 2 above.

GLOSSARY

Most of the German words and a few of the English terms that are discussed in the Prologue or the notes are listed here with references to the pages where the explanation can be found.

abfallen, Abgefallensein, 110n
Ablauf, 106n
act, actual, actuality, actualize, 45f., 61n
alienation, 38, 49, 107n
All, 143n, 151n
Allbeziehung, 155n
an der Welt, 100n
an sich, 100n
Angesicht, 92n
at hand, 69n, 174n
Auftrag, 101n
befahren, 55n
begegnen, Begegnung, 45
Begrifflichkeit, 175n
behold, 61n
"*bei sich*," 100n
being, 46, 67n
Besinnung, etc., 110n
Bestand, 53n
Bestimmtsein, 109n
Bestimmung, 90n, 108n
bewahrt, bewährt, 163n
Bewährung, 152n
Beziehungen, 79n

Beziehungserlebnis, 81n
beziehungsgemäss, 163n
Bindung, 163n
body, 58n
caprice, 108n
confront, 45, 58n
confrontation, 66n
countenance, 92n
destiny, 90n, 108n
direct, 62n, 68n
doom, 59n
drive, 79n
Du, 14f.
ego, 111n, 115n
egocentric, 95n
Eigenmensch, 115n
Eigenwesen, 111n
Eingestaltung, 161n
Einheit, 135n
"*Einungs*"-*Ekstase*, 135n
elektrische Sonne, 120n
embracing, 178n
encounter, 45, 81n
erfahren, Erfahrung, 55n
erfinden, 61n